MANAGING TO SURVIVE

MANAGING TO SURVIVE

How to outsmart the One Minute Manager

JAMES J. SKIVINGTON

JAVELIN BOOKS
POOLE · NEW YORK · SYDNEY

First published in the UK 1987 by Javelin Books,
Link House, West Street, Poole, Dorset, BH15 1LL

Copyright © 1987 James Skivington

Distributed in the United States by
Sterling Publishing Co., Inc.,
2 Park Avenue, New York, NY 10016

Distributed in Australia by
Capricorn Link (Australia) Pty Ltd,
PO Box 665, Lane Cove, NSW 2066

British Library Cataloguing in Publication Data

Skivington, James J.
 Managing to survive : how to outsmart the
 one minute manager.
 1. Management — Great Britain
 I. Title
 658′. 00941   HD70.G7

ISBN 0 7137 1986 9

Typeset by Butler & Tanner Ltd, Frome
Printed in Great Britain by Guernsey Press Co. C.I.

CONTENTS

LIST OF ILLUSTRATIONS

NOTE TO THE READER
(MALE OR FEMALE)

It is an uncomfortable fact of corporate life that most middle and senior executives are male.

There *are* successful and striking exceptions but they are – unfortunately – still exceptions.

Because of this, managers in this book are, in general, referred to as male. This does not reflect on the mental attitude of the author (male) or the author's editor (female) – merely on the business world in general.

INTRODUCTION

Here is the fairy tale: in the corporate jungle there are three groups of animal: the tigers, the goats and the foxes. Now the tigers – who are few – try to make the running in this jungle, roaring in the night to establish both territory and their dominance in it. They are predators of the goats – who are many – these huddle together for protection or flee in terror from the marauding carnivores, stumbling blindly through the commercial undergrowth until they are bloodily devoured or lie safe but exhausted in some departmental thicket. The tigers do devour the odd goat, to keep body and soul together, but their reputation is mainly established by their striking appearance, the loudness of their voices and their dynamic movements, even though the latter rarely produce any effective action. The goats know that they can never be tigers and as they wish dominance over nobody, their only desire is to be left in peace, to get on with their simple lives. Sadly, they are natural victims and are inherently ignorant in the ways of the jungle.

Being a fox is a different matter entirely. The fox can never be a tiger, although he may sometimes misguidedly wish to be one, but neither is he willing to be a goat. The fox is an intelligent survivor. He practises his ways deep in the undergrowth or under cover of darkness; he knows all the holes through which he can slip undetected and his sharp eyes miss nothing. He does not prey on the goats – for they present no threat to him except when they collectively bolt, and then he will always have a bolt-hole.

The tiger knows that the fox is both unappetising and capable of retaliation if cornered, so he leaves him well alone. While the tiger may die of over-exertion and the goat of fright, the fox, because of his knowledge and its judicious application, survives long after the tigers and the goats have gone. This book is about being a fox.

1 THE RELUCTANT MANAGER

'Never put off till tomorrow what you can do today because you might do it today and like it and want to do it again tomorrow.'

Plato

It may be that you were reasonably happy as a manager in your organisation; for many people are quite content with their lot. You may not have been the highest paid or the recipient of the best conditions, but you could do the job competently and were well thought of by boss and colleagues alike. It would not have been the end of the world if you had to stay in that position until you retired. At least you could look forward to many pleasant years free from stress and harassment. Then you stumble on a review of management position in an upmarket Sunday paper and later buy the book because it is highly recommended by a colleague with a vicious sense of humour. The book is of the 'How to become President of General Motors in Three Easy Lessons' variety. Suddenly you realise how little you know. Failure and opprobrium loom menacingly ahead. What is 'peer group pressure'? What are 'T-groups' and 'quality circles'? And what about Theories X, Y and Z? You have plotted your management style on a matrix, and now discover that it is not what you thought it was, and that anyway you can't understand the description of what it is supposed to be . . .

After this your view of the job you do and how you carry it out can never be quite the same again. Slowly it becomes clear that certain assumptions are made about you, as they are about many people in management, i.e.

- your overweening ambition in life is to claw your way to the top/carve out a niche for yourself/make your mark in management (note that these are all essentially destructive activities)
- you hunger after money and power and have set your sights on becoming chief executive at the earliest possible opportunity

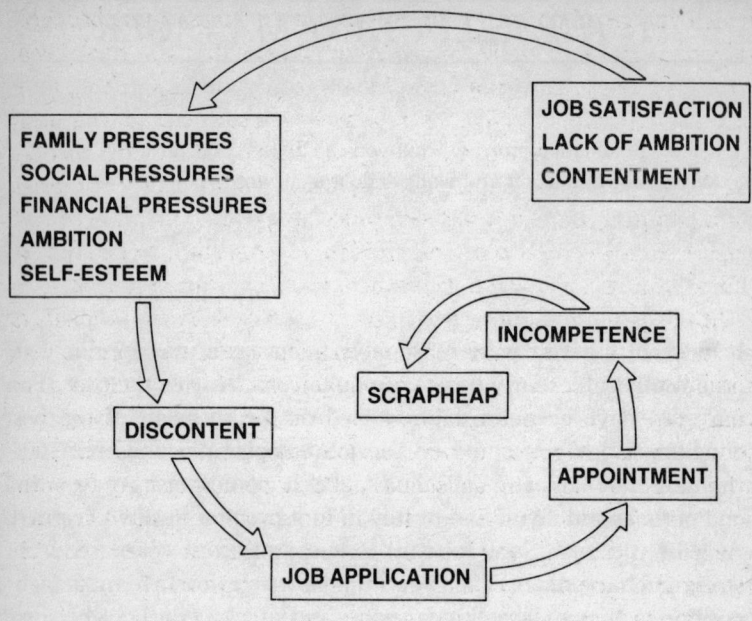

- you are quite willing to sacrifice your family, friends and principles to get what you want
- given the right conditions you are capable of being utterly ruthless

Everyone else thinks this way and therefore so must you, otherwise you are branded as being:

- a lunatic
- a liar
- a Communist
- all three

Of course, you resist: you are your own man, after all. Yet despite your resolve you are now set on a hazardous new course through unfamiliar and uncharted waters. Suddenly you seem to have lost your old confidence in your decision-making ability; courses of action that previously never cost you a moment's thought now seem fraught with danger; and you find that advertisements for highly paid jobs which you could do with your eyes closed are increasingly brought to your attention. Finally the realisation dawns that you have been wrong all along. Far from being happy with your lot working in a pleasant department of a fine company with a caring boss, you now realise that you are actually working for a hick outfit which is merely exploiting your good nature and capacity for hard work in return for a pittance. Socially, you begin to feel inadequate and it becomes apparent that your spouse and children are reluctant to be seen in public with you and will only travel in your 'old' car after dark.

At this point you are approaching an irrevocable commitment to get yourself a better managerial position in a prestige company or risk divorce, career failure and social ostracism. The plain fact is now that even if your organisation was to make you chief executive tomorrow *and* offer you a lucrative share deal, you would not stay with them. What have satisfaction and happiness got to do with anything? You are a manager and this is your career. And if you are going to succeed (a word purposely left undefined by those who require the success of you), you had better equip yourself for the task by learning how to become a management fox.

2 FINDING THE JOB

'Give me a tool and I'll give him a job.'

Winston Churchill

There are many ways of managing to get a job, just as there are many ways of managing *not* to get one, the latter skill being found in abundance among those from both ends of the social scale who have made a career out of pursuing their leisure activities. Perhaps it is not surprising, bearing in mind the results that some of them produce, that quite a few senior managers are in this socio-economic group, and although you may well aspire to it yourself it is worth noting that only a small percentage of hopefuls ever succeed. At least in the initial stages you must content yourself with managing to survive, and, as a prerequisite for this, finding the right job. The principal methods of doing so are set out in the following pages.

ADVERTISEMENTS

You apply to a newspaper or magazine advertisement placed directly by the recruiting company or by 'recruitment consultants'. Great care is needed in your initial reading of these advertisements. Some of them are strictly accurate and honest, telling you all you could possibly want to know, while others are grossly misleading, either deliberately or through the incompetence of the person who drafted them. Some are so vague that they could be offering almost any kind of financial deal, ranging from you paying them for the privilege of working in their company, to a six-figure salary with two cars and health insurance for your pets. The job might be as a sales manager, farm labourer or astro-physicist and it could be based anywhere between Reykjavik and Rangoon. In every case you can be sure that the company will be 'a market leader' and is 'expanding' and 'innovative'. Companies which have marketing problems, flagging sales and inefficient production methods apparently never need to advertise for managers.

- If the advertisement reveals a number of vacancies in the same company, this is a cause for some concern: it may indicate that a mass walkout of staff has occurred, leaving the pieces to be picked up by the successful applicants.
- No matter how desperate you are to obtain a job, do not write to the company saying, 'I would like to apply for the position of Sales Director. If I am held to be unsuitable or this position has already been filled, I would be equally interested in the vacancy for a boilerman.'
- Beware of those advertisements which state, 'must be self-starter', or 'must be capable of working on own initiative'. These are normally euphemisms for 'no training, assistance or co-operation will be forthcoming from any quarter'. If a 'self-starter with a first-class track record' is required, you can be sure that you will have to do everything on your own and at the pace of an Olympic sprinter.

In order to find out more details about a poorly-described vacancy, e.g. job location, salary, it may sometimes be possible to telephone the company and elicit information from a junior member of the Personnel Department by saying that you are from the Job Centre, or that you are a departmental head in a sister company which has an employee interested in the vacancy. To discover the finer details of a vacancy advertised by recruitment consultants, find out the name of an employee at another branch of their company, then use it when telephoning the advertising branch. If you have detailed knowledge of a particular industry you may be able to narrow down to a handful the number of companies likely to be advertising, then telephone each one until you find the one which has placed the advertisement. Tracking down these retiring companies is a good test of your initiative and can be fun. It is up to you to try and find out what lies between the lines. Do bear in mind that most job advertisements are:

- dictated on the telephone by a semi-literate manager who only decided ten minutes beforehand to recruit a new member of staff

- lovingly and lengthily constructed, with due consideration for the visual and psychological impact of the advertisement on potential applicants, by a graduate personnel officer who does not know the first thing about the job he is advertising
- written in a recruitment agency by a consultant using a standard job description. He has never been to the company and does not know the first thing about the job

DIRECT APPLICATION

The technique of applying to a company 'on spec' can often be useful if your letter is lucky enough to coincide with their need for someone with your experience. Keep the letter short and to the point, stressing in it the main achievements in your career (which does not include hanging on to your present job through thick and thin).

As with all forms of job application, if you are unemployed avoid saying so, as some employers seem to regard this as a kind of contagious social disease which somehow disqualifies the applicant for further useful work. Use alternative phrases such as 'taking a sabbatical', 'lengthy illness due to overwork', or 'management research'. Remember you are selling yourself and you have only one chance with each employer, so make it good. If a large company is suitably impressed by someone who has applied to them directly they may offer him employment even although they do not currently have a vacancy. Caution is needed here. You may end up with a well-paid non-job with a long title, supposedly temporary, and end up in a corporate backwater.

An alternative to direct application by letter is the direct telephone approach to the chief executive. This can sometimes bear fruit if you have the personality and technique to carry it off. He may be impressed that you were able to find out his name, get through a battery of switchboards and secretaries and track him down to his office or golf club (try obtaining his private number by telephoning his secretary, saying you are from his stockbrokers and that unfortunately your computer files have been wiped). Once through to the great man, give him a plausible and unverifiable reason for your approach, e.g. a friend told you the company was looking for someone with just your background and experience, or that after exhaustive study of his company's recent performance you feel you could make a vital contribution in certain areas. Vaguely mention large increases in sales, decreases in costs and such like. Given the power and unshakeable belief in their own judgement that some chief executives have, they can often decide on a whim to give you an interview ... after that, it's up to you. Whatever you do, do not attempt to contact him at home: he may not have admitted to his wife that he is a director of the company.

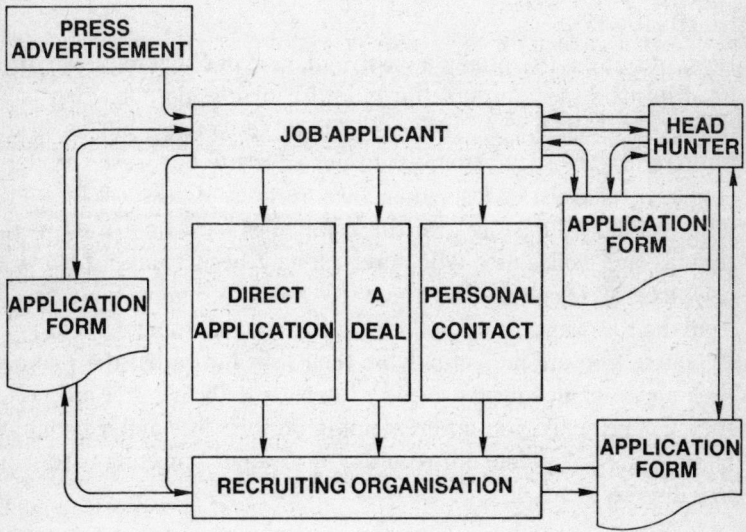

PERSONAL CONTACTS

Do not be afraid to ask favours from influential friends or embarrass them into assisting you to find a suitable position:

- apologise for being late for a social event because you had to drop your wife off in the red light district
- brag that your wife has taken a job in a coal-mine, 'just for the experience'
- ask them if they have any old clothes for sale

Make promises if you must – you can always go back on them later. You may lose a friend this way, but you may also get yourself a first-class job, and which one of them pays the bills?

One of the great advantages of getting a job through personal contacts is that it often cuts out all the laborious work of writing letters, filling in inane application forms and being subjected to aggressive interviews. Moreover, if your contact is highly connected you will have the additional bonus of an inside line on board decisions, enabling you to keep one step ahead of your fellow competitors in the organisation.

HEAD HUNTERS

Head hunting is essentially a passive method of obtaining a job: the head hunters seek you out (or, more frequently, do not when you think that they should). It is desirable to get yourself put on head hunters' lists as they generally do not advertise but work through contacts, referrals, or from their own records. If possible, find out who the individuals are and the companies for whom they work (friends and colleagues who have already been head-hunted are useful here), telephone them and ask them to remove your name from their lists as you are no longer interested in changing your job. Of course, you are not actually on their lists, but rather than admit their apparent incompetence and lose a potentially lucrative prospect, they will persuade you into remaining on their lists and ask you to fill in forms 'to up-date our records', or arrange a meeting with you in a discreet location.

A DEAL

It may sometimes be possible to manoeuvre a private arrangement with a supplier or customer of your present company, whereby a transaction which is advantageous to them is carried out in return for your joining them in a management position after a suitable period of time has elapsed. This is by no means an uncommon happening but requires a discreet approach. If possible, you should manoeuvre the conversation so that the other party makes the first move. In this deal it is essential that nothing is committed to writing and that absolute confidentiality is assured from both sides.

Knowledge is a valuable commodity at all times but especially in the context of a deal. It can be used to obtain a managerial position in another company, or indeed promotion in your present one, e.g.

- catching your boss in a compromising position with his secretary
- finding out that he has fiddled the sales or production figures
- discovering that he has been syphoning petrol out of his company car and putting it in his wife's car

In extremis, other methods which are worth a try are:
- sob story: you need extra money for your sick grandmother (this will not work with the majority of chief executives as they have probably already sold their grandmothers and are incapable of any emotional response in this area); you can't afford a new tyre for your Porsche
- bribery: a job in return for a consideration (be imaginative!)
- actual, or threats of, physical violence: this is not recommended unless the man is considerably older and smaller than you and has recently been ill

Of course, this list is not exhaustive. Incidentally, if you try either of the last two methods you may well end up in jail – where you will have ample time to think up other approaches.

THE APPLICATION FORM

The dreaded application form is less a request for information than an obstacle course cunningly designed to:

- test your physical and mental stamina
- trap you into embarrassing admissions and omissions
- make you feel inadequate because you cannot remember which years you started/finished school/college/university; cannot remember the dates of birth of your children; have no interesting hobbies like underwater chess or elephant racing

It may be possible to avoid filling in an application form if you send a comprehensive CV to the company first. Usually, however, on receipt of your CV they will send you an application form so that you can while away a few happy hours filling in the same details on that. This is to test your mettle and see if you are really interested in working for a company which can only absorb data in a pre-determined format. Forget about having a CV 'professionally presented' or the like. All this means is that the company who do it for you will use fancy notepaper, a brown typewriter ribbon, put it in a glossy folder and charge you a fat fee for the privilege. Most companies are so fed up with these pieces of hype that they will be the first to be picked out of the pile and thrown to one side without being read. Far better to have your CV typed or neatly written on plain paper. Your sterling qualities and sound experience will still come shining through.

Often an application form will request that you fill it in 'in your own handwriting' (as if you would get someone else to fill it in for you!). If your handwriting is poor, get someone else to fill the form in for you, then wear an armsling to the interview, if you get one. The reason that companies request this is that it is a well-known fact that poor writers are invariably poor managers.

The first information usually required on a job application form is personal details: name, address, age, spouse's occupation, etc. Bear in mind the following points:

Name:

Even this can catch you out if you are not careful. If one of your given names is outlandish/highly unusual/silly, then miss it out completely. You would be amazed at the things which put an employer off a job applicant. Of course, there is not much you can do about your surname. With a name like Colin Robert Allan Pritchard, always write it out in full: do not simply write down the initials.

Address:

Anyone who values their privacy might well consider putting a Post Office box number in here.

Age:

If you think it will help you, feel free to lie about your age (though 'over 21' won't do). However, this can be fraught with danger as you must carefully work out the dates when you should have been at school and in each job, as well as remembering what age you are supposed to be when you go for the interview. This may well be worthwhile when you are outside the age range which the advertisement states – 'age indicator' is the euphemism sometimes used. It is a well-known fact that anyone over the age of 38 is decrepit, senile and unfit for any kind of useful employment.

Spouse's occupation:

It may be better to skip this one, rather than having to admit to some occupation such as 'runs a flea circus' or, even worse, 'tax inspector'. On the other hand, 'wine and spirits buyer' might just swing you the job.

Depending on what they are, you may be able to add to or exaggerate qualifications that you have legitimately. Most companies don't check up on these and would not look askance on a Fellow of the Royal College of Surgeons with a Ph.D. in Serbo-Croat working as a Production Control Manager. If you are a bit short on qualifications, make up a few, e.g. Licentiate of the Institute of Electricians (LIE), Fellow of the Institute of Buyers (FIB), or any other combination that takes your fancy. The company will not want to admit their ignorance by asking what the letters mean. If they do, and they say they have never heard of the qualification, tell them that you obtained it by correspondence course from a college in Peru which has since gone into liquidation.

Filling in the 'previous experience' section on an application form can be very tricky. Your object here is to convey a picture of:

- continuity of employment
- steady progression up the managerial ladder
- new challenges and learning in each job

Again, a considerable degree of creative writing can be employed here, as long as you can back it up convincingly in the interview but, for instance, do not claim extensive computer experience simply because you never get fouled up on your bank's cash dispenser. Embellish the details of the jobs you have had by using the most technical-sounding terms, e.g. not 'stock control' but 'inventory control'; 'Materials Requirements Planning', not 'progress chasing'; 'architecturalist', in place of 'window-cleaners'.

If one of your jobs only lasted six months because you and your boss did not see eye to eye (i.e. you did not agree with him firing you), put it down as a short term contract job, with an explanation such as 'I wanted to take some time out to consider the next move in my long term career path before committing myself to a permanent position'. 'Reasons for leaving the job' can be many and varied.

Putting 'moving home' can be a good one. Even if you did not actually move home you can say that your spouse changed his/her mind after you had handed in your resignation. Writing 'more money' as a reason for leaving is pointless. If they are worth their salt, the company to whom you are applying will make sure that you do not come out on top in salary negotiations, and in any event they are probably looking for an idealist who regards money as coming a long way behind hard work and service to the company.

Ensure that there are no significant time gaps in your list of former jobs, otherwise the company will assume that you were:

- unemployed
- in jail
- attending a rehabilitation centre

If you cannot avoid showing a prolonged period of unemployment, use your imagination and come up with something unusual. For example, a man could claim a role reversal experiment with his wife; a woman can claim a false pregnancy.

Do not be backward about exaggerating your former jobs and your achievements. After all, the company have probably done the same in their job advertisement, e.g.

- 'market leader'
- 'unique product'
- 'challenging opportunity'
- 'substantial salary commensurate with the position'

Do not forget that they are trying to sell themselves to you and are not going to tell you that they are struggling and need an experienced and tough-minded manager such as yourself to turn the company back from the brink, while the chairman keeps well out of the way in case anyone notices those qualities in him that got the company into the mess in the first place.

If the job advertisement shows no company name, location, or salary, and is otherwise vague, you would probably be best to forget about the whole thing. Most companies are more than happy to take the opportunity of putting their name in big type beside a good job with a decent salary; it shows that they are active in bringing fresh blood into the organisation and it also helps to keep their name before their customers. If there are no details on the advertisement, ask yourself what they have got to hide.

Virtually every application form has columns on it for 'Salary: start/finish', but how are you supposed to remember what you earned fifteen years ago (except that you know it was not enough)? You've guessed it, you will have to make it up. Since it was a long time ago, your salary would have been very small, given your career progression since then, and the inflation which so badly affected prices whilst leaving your salary relatively unscathed. Having decided upon your first salary, continue year by year, awarding yourself steady pay increases until you reach your present salary. This will indicate a steady if unspectacular career progression, which will appear very satisfactory, as most companies are conservative and likely to get the wind up if they think they have a budding entrepreneur on their hands – after all, he might be smarter than the boss.

When it comes to your present salary, add everything in: expenses, performance, bonuses, luncheon vouchers, health insurance, and the monetary equivalent of your company car (be liberal). At the interview you can refer to this figure as 'the total package' (you should take every opportunity to use their jargon to your advantage). If you say, 'Oh, and I have a company car with the job', the chances are that they will assume this is in addition to the figure you have quoted.

You may discover that the salary in the job advertisement, in common with the company and job descriptions, has been grossly exaggerated and that in order to earn the stated amount, which is largely performance bonus, you would need to have the speed and stamina of Superman. Anything with 'salary commensurate with experience' in the advertisement is hardly worth pursuing: guess who'll be evaluating your experience?

One final word on salary. Never fill in the 'Expected salary range' section. If your expected salary range comes within the company's budgeted figure they will simply knock off 10 per cent and offer you that. Are they paying you what you are worth or the amount on which you can manage to survive?

The filling in of the 'Hobbies and pastimes' section on an application form is normally erroneously regarded as unimportant, but do not be misled. An applicant's hobbies can be very revealing and can greatly assist the company in its assessment of him or her. For example, someone putting down his pastimes as music, reading, gardening and necromancy, might well lead the employer to deduce that he was not the staid citizen that he might otherwise appear. Anything to do with politics or protest groups is definitely out, as is anything unusual or intellectual; e.g., if you give 'classical music' as a pastime they are likely to put you down as an impractical dreamer incapable of holding down a dynamic managerial position. Foreign interests of any sort are usually regarded with suspicion and lead to an assumption that the applicant is lacking in patriotism. Of course, this need not necessarily be the case if you are applying to a subsidiary of a foreign company in this country, although paradoxically you will often find that such companies try to give the appearance of being the most patriotic of all: 'Support home industry, buy Zanvolvich'.

In the matter of hobbies, however, you must put something down. If you leave this section blank the company will conclude that:

- you have something to hide, which is bad
- you have nothing to hide, which is worse
- you never keep any hobby more than two weeks

Try and get a balanced group of pastimes, in order to reflect your balanced personality, making sure that you include a sport of some kind, even if your idea of exercise is grating cheese on a pizza. Do not forget to read up on your chosen sport before the interview, because the chances are that if you have written 'lacrosse', the interviewing Chairman or Managing Director will have been captain of his college or university team.

Trick questions appear in a variety of guises on job application forms, a common one being 'What is the state of your health?' Just try putting 'occasional migraine headaches' and see what kind of job that gets you. Writing 'good' in this section will not get you anywhere either, as you will doubtless be confronted with it at the interview.

'I see you have put down your health as "good"?'

'Yes. It's generally okay, I'm glad to say.'

'How do you know it's good? Are you a doctor?'

'Well, no, but . . .'

'I mean, how do you know there's not something ... serious happening inside you right now?'

'I ... don't ...'

'I think we'd better put your health down as 'doubtful', don't you?'

Another question of this type is 'Have you a criminal record?' Do not write, 'I didn't know I needed one for this position', as it will only antagonise the person reading the form. On the other hand, if you are applying for the post of manager in a security company, personal protection company or second-hand car dealer's, give all details of your convictions as this may well assist you in obtaining the job.

THE STING IN THE TAIL

This feature is becoming more commonplace in application forms; it is the section headed 'Please give a résumé of your career to date and say how you see it developing in the future'. It is very easy to spend hours on this, writing and rewriting your attempts on separate sheets of paper, as you weigh each word and phrase in an effort to do yourself justice without going over the top. But there is no need for this résumé to read like a book blurb. What is required is a set of simple, clear statements of the high points in your career (suitably embellished, of course), and no more than two firm objectives for the future, which should be vague enough not to compromise you and specific enough to be credible. One sentence should suffice for this, with phrases such as 'broadening my skill and knowledge' and 'taking on more responsibility'. Stating wild and impractical ambitions such as 'becoming a divisional or company director' is out, as you will merely be seen as a troublemaker and a potential threat to the status quo.

Application forms can and do vary, so read and reread them several times before committing anything to paper, keeping an eye out for doubtful meanings, or provocative trick questions designed to trap the unwary. Remember, the less you give away, the stronger your position. And finally, don't forget to take a copy of your application form/CV before you send it off: it will not improve your chances of getting the job if at the interview the man with your application form knows more about you than you do.

3 THE INTERVIEW

'If you must be caught with your trousers down, at least make sure you are facing in the right direction.'

Nietzsche

A job interview need not be traumatic if you give it some thought beforehand and take time to prepare for it by reading up on key facts about the company, e.g. annual sales, markets, products, parent company and so forth. Best of all, if you know someone who works in the company you can pump him for information. Try and find out such things as how the advertised job came to be vacant, how many people have been in the job in the last three or four years, what your prospective boss is really like, e.g. is he:

- neurotic?
- an alcoholic?
- incompetent?
- a womaniser (and if so, are there any decent-looking women left in the company)?
- all four of the above (in which case his early demise may allow you to step into a plum job)?

Always remember, the best kind of information in management, as in life, is inside information, as anything worth keeping quiet is worth finding out, especially if the person attempting to keep it quiet does not realise that you know it.

The cardinal point, which you must hold before you at the interview, is that you are evaluating the company every bit as much as they are evaluating you. Arm yourself with specific questions, but avoid anything nasty or underhand like 'Do you mind if I talk to some of your customers to see what their opinion is of your company?' If you are being interviewed by the Chairman or Managing Director, be careful not to make the questions too tough as this will only lead to embarrassment. Apart from knowing the name of the organisation and its main products or services, he probably will not know much more, so do not ask things like 'How many people work here?' (He will almost certainly say 'About half of them.') 'What was the turnover per employee last year? What was the gross and net profit?' If you have done your homework, you will be able to tell him, because you will have read the company's annual report, whereas he will merely have signed it!

Whatever people may say about them, first impressions do count and appearance is important. Be conservative in what you wear to the interview; lavender suede boots and a canary-yellow waistcoat might indicate a vibrant personality but will hardly convince the interviewer of your managerial prowess. Most directors and senior managers are conservative people, even though they may have very exotic tastes in private life (which they will be at great pains to keep private). If you are in the habit of wearing jewellery it would be best if you left it off, as a diamond stud in the ear or nose might appear offensive, and half a pound of gold bracelet shooting out from under your shirt cuff when you reach out to shake hands might unnerve an elderly chairman.

The car which you drive to the interview could make or mar your chances. If you arrive in something which looks as if it came last in a stock car race and sounds like the gunfight at the OK Corral, this will not do much for your dynamic managerial image. Park it out of sight of the company and walk to the building. In some instances an especially favourable impression can be created by hiring a luxury car for the day, but if you do so, make sure the person interviewing you knows about it, by saying 'It is all right to park my Porsche/Mercedes/Jaguar over there, isn't it?' Check, however, on the parking spaces marked 'Chairman' and 'Managing Director' before you enter the building. If your car is better than either of theirs, keep off the subject of cars completely.

Companies and individuals use many different interviewing techniques, ranging from the wholly structured interview, using forms to rate the interviewee's attributes, to the highly unstructured ramblings of the man who seems to love the sound of his own voice and thinks that he is the best interviewer since the Spanish Inquisition. There may be one person interviewing you or several, and although the latter situation is grossly unfair (would they like it if you brought along four friends to help you answer the questions which are put to you?), there is not a lot you can do about it. Fortunately, the majority of interviewers are incompetent, as interviewing, like so many other management techniques, is supposed to come naturally

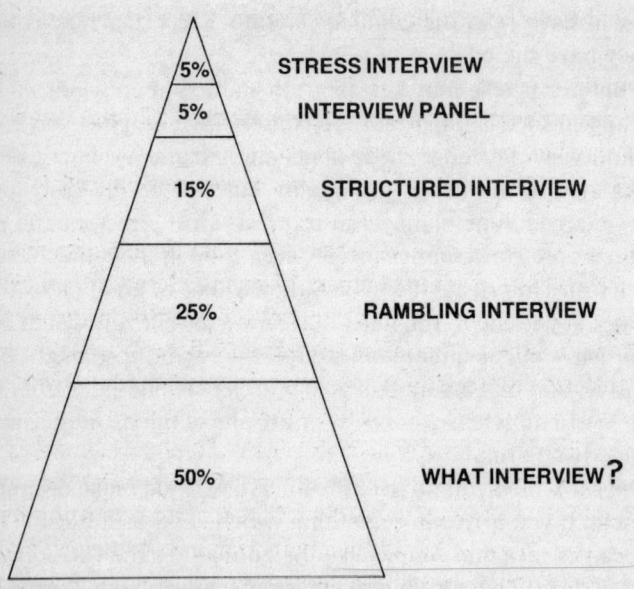

to all mature and intelligent managers. If the interviewer starts the interview by saying 'Would you have a pen I could borrow?' then you know that with a bit of luck you can tie him in knots. In such a case, be bold. Dominate the conversation and steer it towards those areas in which you are strongest. Question the interviewer unceasingly; not only should this give you vital information but it will not allow him any time for questioning you. When you have learned all that you want to know, stand up abruptly, say, 'Thank you very much. I'll be in touch with you shortly,' and leave the room.

A particularly nasty form of interrogation is the so-called 'stress interview', but due to the number of interviewers left holding their bleeding noses, this is now less common than before. Nevertheless, you may still be subjected to a stress interview and the kind of thing you can expect is:

- the office door knob coming off in your hand
- being asked to take a seat when there is none
- the chair you are given being at least 2 ft below that of the interviewer
- being asked how you take your coffee and then being brought tea, without the milk which you take in tea but do not take in coffee
- having tea spilt over you
- someone in the next room attacking the wall with an electric drill which only you seem to hear
- the interviewer being consistently and extremely rude

Of course, it may be that such things are due to incompetence and do not constitute a planned stress interview. Stress interviews are normally the product of a large corporation's Personnel department, which has a surfeit of graduate personnel officers who must justify their existence by thinking up ever more outlandish ways of torturing innocent interviewees. Their other speciality is the written test.

Generally, there is no forewarning of a written test and it is sprung on you at the interview. It can take the form of an aptitude and/or personality test, although it will not be called that. It will probably have a foreign name or the name of some well-known business school. All of these pseudo-scientific tests are useless at predicting anything – except that the person who invents/administers/interprets them will get grossly overpaid for sitting around saying 'On the one hand ...' and 'On the other hand ...'. If you suspect that you may be asked to take such a test, wear your arm in a sling when attending for interview or, if caught unawares, then work through the test from the beginning, putting the answer to the first question against the last question, the second against the second last and so on. This will confuse all of them beyond measure and your test will be discounted. Alternatively, you could look at the small print at the bottom of the last page, where you will probably discover the year in which the test was published. If it is more than two years old (some companies actually believe that what was strongly advocated by experts two years ago is still valid!), draw the attention of the interviewer to this, saying 'But this is hopelessly out of date. Haven't you got the latest one, the Muttelpunk-Hochenschnauzer Ability and Aptitude Predictor?' Acutely embarrassed, the interviewer will withdraw the test he has given you and make no more mention of it. Thus, in doing yourself a favour, you may simultaneously strike a blow for democracy by getting the test administrator fired.

With the test out of the way, you now move into the main body of the interview. As this can take any one of a dozen forms, it is difficult to prepare yourself by formulating a course of action or line of argument, but there are basic principles which apply regardless of the interviewer or his style. However nervous and desperate you are, never ask to be allowed to smoke during an interview when it is obvious that none of the others in the room wish to do so. On the other hand, if the interviewer offers you a cigarette and you do not smoke, take one immediately, in order to reassure him that it is not the filthy habit he knows it is. Assure him that you are planning a major increase in your cigarette consumption and then join him in a good cough. You will probably have made a friend for life (however long that lasts).

It is important that during the interview you keep a sense of proportion, especially if you are keen to get the job after it has been described in glowing terms. Do not over-commit yourself. Yes, you will do a good workmanlike job, but you will not:

- transform in three months the bad worker/management relations of ten years' standing
- raise productivity by 50 per cent while at the same time introducing a whole new product range and slashing raw materials inventory, work in progress and finished goods inventory
- dramatically increase product quality using production machinery which would have been an embarrassment to the men who built the pyramids
- fire a trade union troublemaker who has worked in the company for twenty years and whom nobody has had the guts to fire in all that time

They must be joking! Remember, you did not even want the job in the first place.

As the interview progresses and you are taken for a tour of the premises it may become increasingly obvious that you have been brought there under false pretences; the company is not a leader in its industry, its products/services are third rate, and the managing director knows as much about management as a Trappist monk. Say nothing of this until towards the end of the interview when you collect your travelling expenses (if they do not offer any, force them into giving you some by saying that you got them at a rival company the previous week). Once you have the money safely in your pocket you can go to town regarding misrepresentation: in all your born days you've never seen such a hick outfit; you wouldn't work there if it was the last job in the world; at those wages it should be classified as charity work, etc. At this stage you have nothing to lose, and it will do wonders for your ego, which is, if you remember, the most important thing in management.

Ending an interview, like closing a sale, is always a tricky but important part of the procedure. Do not say wimpish things like 'I hope to see you again soon,' nudge, wink; 'I feel sure that if I was fortunate enough to be offered this position I could make a significant contribution to the profitability and success of the company.' It is far better to say something like 'There are obviously quite a number of points for me to consider. You should hear from me in about a week, when I will have interviewed a number of other companies and will be in a position to make a decision.' Whatever happens, do not let them think they have you in the palm of their hand – even if they do.

Now all you have to do is sit back and wait for the job offer. If you get a letter saying that the vacancy has now been filled, that presents no problems. After all, you did not want the job in the first place. You will often find that the company has not got the basic good manners to reply at all. If they have not written after a reasonable period has elapsed, write them a letter thanking them for their attendance at the interview and stating that there were a considerable number of candidate companies and unfortunately theirs was not short-listed for further consideration; however, you will keep their details on file and if you are every really desperate, you will get in touch with them.

When you do receive a letter or a telephone call making you a job offer, do not rush to accept. Take time to decide, if only to let the company know that you are not at their beck and call. Question the details of the offer, and try and get them to commit themselves to improvements in it, e.g.

- 'Is the salary figure quoted per month or per annum?'
- 'I've been offered another job at twice the salary you are offering, but I may take your job for the experience.'
- 'Due to commitments at my present company, I will not be able to take up the appointment for another month.'
- 'As I have no wish to distract the workers at a critical phase in their work cycle, it has long been my practice to start work at around 10.30 each morning.'

Until you receive a written offer from the company, never give them your acceptance of a job, otherwise you may find that details of salary, bonuses and other benefits are fudged and they will later deny all knowledge of having offered you what you claim.

It is often a good idea to get yourself some interviews simply for practice, if you have not attended one for some time. Not only will this sharpen your technique but it can be quite enjoyable, as you will be able to sit with your feet on the chairman's desk, pick your teeth with a matchstick, ask stupid questions and then interrupt the answer, etc. There is no reason why you should not waste the company's time: they would be quite willing to waste yours by having you as a make-weight when the job had already been promised to someone in the company. If you remember that companies are primarily interested in their own welfare and not yours, you will not go far wrong. By attempting to screw them you can only earn their respect, as this is the only *modus operandi* they know. They will fling out their arms and greet you like a long-lost brother, welcoming you into the corporate fold in recognition of your undoubted management prowess. At last! that management job which you never wanted is yours.

4 GET ORGANISED

'I know that $E = mc^2$, but Brother, I'll never understand dames.'

Albert Einstein

Now that you have become a member of a leading organisation, it might be as well if you knew something about organisational theory. This subject should give no cause for concern, however, as most of it can be dismissed out of hand. Entrepreneurs may sit around building corporations in the air, replete with corporate strategies, organisational charts and goals, but ultimately what makes organisations function, or not, is individual managers with personal goals. Corporate goals can only be entertained insofar as they accord with the individual aspirations of managers. So, if you remember nothing else about organisations, remember one thing: egos are far and away the most important motivating force.

Nevertheless, in order to understand why companies are organised in the way that they are, let us briefly survey some of the main organisational and management theories and the culprits who advanced them. One of the earliest was an American, F. W. Taylor (1856–1917), who was called 'the father of scientific management'. He has since been called other names but these are not relevant here. Amongst other things, Taylor developed and advocated 'work measurement', 'work specialisation' and, his *pièce de résistance*, 'functional management'. This latter method of management required that each supervisor in an organisation should have a specialist role, with the effect that a worker might receive orders from up to eight supervisors, depending on the task to be carried out. Apart from a considerable increase in the rate of mental breakdown amongst workers, there was no noticeable effect on industrial efficiency from the application of this theory. Need we say anything more about Frederick Winslow Taylor?

A French mining engineer, Henri Fayol (1841–1925), put forward the theory that industrial organisations could engage in six types of activities, and undertake five types of action, governed by fourteen principles. This gives us five hundred and twenty possible management scenarios (perhaps this is why it takes so long to get a decision out of anyone in management nowadays). Fayol also advocated the use of organisation charts, presumably after his '520 scenarios' idea went down like a lead balloon. The organisation chart has been very widely adopted throughout all sizes and types of bureaucratic, commercial and industrial organisations, to the extent that you can walk into any one of them at any time and be given a precise and detailed chart of what the organisational structure was four years ago on a day on which the chief executive could find nothing better to occupy himself.

Max Weber (1864–1920), despite being an academic all his life and a German lawyer to boot, decided that this management business was pretty straightforward stuff and came up with the theory that there are three types of authority, i.e. 'bureaucratic', 'traditional' and 'charismatic'. Unfortunately, organisations did not beat a path to his door with offers of lucrative management positions as a result of these revelations.

Another academic, the American Mary Parker Follett (1863–1933), proposed that 'the law of the situation' should determine what action is taken when a managerial problem arises. Orders, she said, should be the composite decision of those who give and those who receive them. It is not known if Ms Follett subsequently went on to make a comfortable living as a humourist.

Elton Mayo (1880–1949) was an Australian who started out as a medical student and then switched to philosophy and psychology. He conducted the famous Hawthorne studies in the USA in 1927. These consisted of studying six girls in the relay assembly test room in the Western Electric Company for one and a half years. After resting from this arduous task, he undertook the study of eighteen people in the Bank Wiring Observation Room and discovered that the group's social structure was 'an intricate web of human relations bound together by a system of sentiments' and that there was an informal organisation made up of groups. Both of these studies took a total of five years, and later Mayo was at a loss to explain why it had taken him so long to find out what every school kid has learned a week after starting school. However, having discovered his talent for spinning out projects, he naturally moved into management consultancy. Latterly, he was a consultant on industrial problems to the British government – given the post-war record of British industry, he obviously knew as much about that as he did about workers on the shop floor.

Coming more up to date let us briefly consider the theories of Douglas McGregor, an American social psychologist. In his famous book *The Human Side of Enterprise* (1960), he put forward 'Theory X' and 'Theory Y' (this may sound like the beginning of a soap advertisement but it's not). 'Theory X' assumes that the worker is lazy and does not like work, that he is unambitious and must be directed at all times. 'Theory Y' claims that people are ambitious, willing to work for the right objectives but are made to be like 'Theory X' by the nature of organisations (which Mayo said were made up of informal groups of . . . workers). Still confused? After publication of his book, there was no mass reorganisation of companies across the nation and radical changes in management methods were not observed as prominent phenomena.

A French mathematician, Graicunas, found his way into the ranks of the management theorists by proposing a formula to determine the number of relationships within a manager's 'span of control'. The formula is:

$$N = \frac{2N}{2} XN - 1$$

where N equals the number of subordinates. But do not try going to your boss and telling him that you cannot run your department because a French mathematician's calculations prove that you have too many people reporting to you! The next thing you'll be calculating will be your severance pay. After all, would you let a French mathematician run your department? Would you let a French mathematician run anything?

In addition to the theorists mentioned above, there have been many others crowding the lucrative stalls in the management market-place, among them Urwick, Brech, Drucker, Simon, Hertzberg, Likert and Argyris, to name but a handful. Very few of them were ever practising managers at any time in their careers and therefore never experienced having to answer two telephones at once, make a decision on a machine breakdown, redeploy labour because of absenteeism, reschedule the day's deliveries, think up a new lie to tell a customer, answer the managing director's query now, and complete a budget for yet another resubmission all before ten o'clock in the morning. But all this is as nothing to the management theorist: like the star of the silent screen, with one bound he is free of such irrelevancies and has carried you off on his magic managerial carpet to the unattainable land of make-believe. However, these books on organisational and management theory are not entirely useless. The next time you are in your office with an ensemble of ringing telephones and a chorus of irate trade unionists banging on your desk, you could always try driving them away by throwing management books at them. At least if they read them they might then understand why the company is in such a bad state, and leave you in peace.

There is obviously no merit in formal organisation theories such as the Classical Approach, the Human Relations Approach or the Systems Approach (these may at one time have been confused with methods for picking up women), so what are you to do? You must learn the rules and study the structure of the informal organisation and the participants in it, i.e. the tigers, the goats and the foxes. Unfortunately you will not find this information on an organisation chart or have it explained to you by the Personnel Manager. You will have to discover it for yourself, and because of its informal nature, this may be no easy task. But if you intend to survive in any organisation, if you are going to become a fox, then discover it you must.

The informal but rigid systems and practices, which are the foundation of all organisations, operate within the context of the so-called 'corporate culture', which specifies norms and modes of behaviour at all levels. You will ignore these at your peril. Always remember, the primary task of a manager is to become adept in the art of politics, now euphemistically called 'power', 'influence' or even 'networking'. If you fail to acquire this knowledge, everything else will be academic, as you will not be in the organisation for very long. In management, getting involved in the murky world of politics is not a matter of choice: politics *is* management. Actually running an organisation so that an end product or service is produced is a necessary evil, a mere front for intrigue, back-stabbing, double-dealing and one-upmanship. Politics is a dangerous game, with frequent casualties, but one way or another you will become involved, so, if you do not wish to be a goat cowering in a departmental thicket, jump right in there and grab yourself some influence. But, where do you begin?

The first step is to find out who has the influence in the organisation – not the power, but the influence. While power will reside with those positions specified in the formal organisation, the influence will be part of the informal structure. Having power is all very well, but being able to influence the use of that power while carrying off the appearance of an innocent bystander in the game is much more important. Although the type of individual who wields the influence can vary from one organisation to another, it is a universal fact that the single most influential group is that of secretaries: never underestimate them. Of course, not all secretaries have influence, and so you must distinguish between the ones that have it and the ones that do not. Look for the people with real power in the organisation and theirs will be the secretaries who have the influence. Of course, it will not be obvious, because the nature of influence is that it is practised in a devious and underhand way and requires the highest degree of artfulness.

Why do secretaries have such influence? Because of one staggeringly simple fact: that virtually all power-seeking male managers in every kind of organisation are unknowingly motivated by the 'Oedipal regression syndrome', which is part and parcel of all male power-seeking. It is a result of domination by an individual's mother or mother-figure in early life which later causes a reactive and unnatural enlargement of the ego and a compensatory need to dominate others as the individual matures. This renders the victim dictatorial, insensible to reasoning, and an absolute autocrat, although paradoxically he retains the habit, if not the need, of being dominated by a woman. And in the context of work, that woman is very likely to be his secretary.

A secretary will not openly criticise any members of management to her boss, but then she hardly needs to do so. A word, a look, perhaps only a shrug might suffice. When disapproval is expressed it appears to be minor and irrelevant, and although it comes from an acute angle it is nonetheless a bolt of lightning.

'I've just about made up my mind to promote John Jones to Head of Department over at Purchasing.'

'Well, of course, that's up to you, Mr Johnson.'

'You sound as if you don't approve, Mary.'

'Oh, it's not for me to approve or disapprove. I presume he can do the job all right. It's just that ... well ... that tie that he had on at the meeting yesterday, I mean ... anybody that could wear a tie like that ... well.'

'Oh ... of course ... I hadn't finally decided on Jones. It was just a thought, Mary.'

From this moment on you can be sure that Jones's goose is cooked.

As the manager frequently has the need to unburden himself to someone, a role which his mother had previously performed, the secretary can become privy to some very interesting tit-bits, both of a business and a personal kind. Personal information may not be useful in the short term (however interesting it may be!), but it is invaluable for assessing character, and it may be used in an emergency, along the lines of, for example, 'You don't transfer me to market research and I won't spread the word about the bulk purchase of widgets that's now lying in the city dump'.

As well as having great influence over her boss the secretary comes in contact with all sorts of interesting information. Through her are channelled all the telephone calls, letters, telexes and memos to her boss. In this way, not only can you get inside information, but you can get advance inside information, and there is no higher category than this. So, the message is clear: you must cultivate the secretaries of the key men for all you are worth (unless they don't like the style of your ties). If you can tap into such a hotline you will not only survive, you will prosper.

As well as cultivating secretaries, the other thing you must do at an early stage is find yourself a godfather. (In jargon this is now called 'mentorship'.) This may take some time, as you must review all possible candidates to find out their 'track records' and their 'prospectivity rating' in the corporate rat-race. It is rather like backing a horse; if you put your shirt on him and he goes down, you are likely to go with him, so pick a good one. He should be powerful in the organisation, have a good information system going and be ruthless at exploiting other people's weaknesses. This will be the man who will push your case when it is advantageous to do so and support you when times get rough. In return, he will ask that you assist him in achieving his personal goals: 'Stick with me boy and we'll go to the top.' Of course, you are not going all the way but simply hitching a ride, keeping afloat on his buoyancy. The top can be a very uncomfortable place to be. Remember, it's the man above the parapet who gets his head shot off.

You must at all times keep an ear open to the informal information system so that you can try and map the continually shifting sands of corporate politics. (Delegation of virtually all your managerial duties will allow you to concentrate on listening to rumours, sifting fact from fiction, undermining your colleagues and similar essential activities.) At the first signs that your godfather's 'prospectivity rating' in the organisation is diminishing, ditch him and find another. Indeed, if you have been doing your job properly, you will have lined up another one already! Not for nothing is this termed 'Parasitic Progression'.

Needless to say, you should not be averse to promotion simply because your primary aim is to survive as a fox. Sometimes promotion has to be accepted in order to allay suspicion, because you can never be seen to be merely a survivor. This might lead your boss to conclude that you were:

- not ambitious enough for management
- mentally ill
- playing some complex organisational game of double bluff which could make his position vulnerable

So you're satisfied with what you've got? You've been promoted to the level of your competence? What has that got to do with anything? We're talking management here.

As you progress up through the management structure, or at least come into contact with those who have already done so, you will gradually become aware of an astonishing but universal truth: in the words of the song, 'It's not what you do, it's the way that you do it.' It is not the 'what' but the 'how' that matters. Just watch the newly-appointed executive and you'll see what this means: give him about a month at the most and suddenly he is a whirlwind of action. Charts, graphs, memos and plans come streaming from his office; people are moved, some of them to other positions or departments, some of them out the door. New positions are created, machines are moved. Some departments are revamped, some restructured, others are merged. Everywhere there is movement, but is there any action? Sadly, the quickness of the hand deceives the eye, but he does it with such style, with such assurance that he must be correct. And nobody but the most astute notices that six years and three managers further on, one manager's innovations are a previous one's status quo.

This syndrome intensifies the higher up the organisation you go, to the extent that the chief executive, who doesn't know a washer from a washing machine, will commit millions with great style and panache to a project which a blind man running backwards for a bus, and certainly the man in the company stock-room, could see is a white elephant, and be hailed as the saviour of the company and a giant among men. This is known as the 'Reverse Progression Technique', in which the participant, while standing still or going backwards, appears to be going forwards in a swift and decisive manner. 'The Reverse Progression Predictor Factor' can be calculated by using the following formula:

$$RPP = \frac{(I \times V) + S}{D - P}$$

where I = Ignorance (on scale 1–10)

      V = Volubility (on scale 1–10)

      S = Salary (thousands)

      D = Average duration (months) of last 5 jobs/positions

      P = Level of position behind the chief executive which the incumbent holds

A golden rule of management is: 'If you can't make it good, make it flashy'. Study those above you in the organisation. You'll soon get the hang of it.

5 MANAGEMENT AT WORK

'If you laid all the managers in the world end to end they would reach the wrong decision.'

President Eisenhower

MANAGERIAL STYLE

Having spent some time acquiring an in-depth knowledge of organisational practices, you must also fit yourself out with a managerial style and some matching techniques as accessories, so that you may confidently parade yourself before your employers and staff. There are a number of ways of acquiring a managerial style. For instance you can simply look at the various alternatives and adopt the one that takes your fancy; a strutting autocrat, perhaps, or a downtrodden democrat. However, if the one you choose is not your natural style, you may have difficulty in keeping up the pretence. You can of course ask your colleagues, your boss or your staff for their appraisal of your managerial style but they will merely give you wildly differing and inaccurate, not to mention untruthful, assessments which at best will be flattering and at worst be slanderous. It is much better to discover your true style for yourself, and then gradually adapt it to the desired configuration.

The only scientific way to place yourself on the managerial style scale is to use some objective testing method. One such rigorously researched test which has recently been introduced is the 'Survival Quotient Assessor', the elements of which are plotted on the 'SQ Target'. By using this test you can accurately typify your management style in one of four sectors:

– goat
– tiger
– snake
– fox

As your objective is to become a fox and survive in the organisational jungle, you can, in time, adapt your style, re-testing yourself on the SQ Target until you conform to the desired pattern.

The test consists of two groups of questions, the first group being scored on the radius of the target and the second group on the circumference. The formula is then used to calculate your Survival Quotient, with the ultimate objective of reducing the area of the target which your score covers until you hit only the bulls-eye in the middle.

QUESTIONS: Group 1 (1–8 Radius scale)

1) One of your staff is feeling off-colour and cannot accomplish the amount of work required. Would you:
    a) sack him/her on the spot? (2 marks)
    b) tell him/her to rest for half an hour? (1 mark)
    c) tell him/her not to bother you as you have more important things to worry about? (0 marks)

2) How often should salary reviews for your staff be carried out?
    a) once every six months? (2 marks)
    b) once a year? (1 mark)
    c) never? (0 marks)

3) First thing in the morning, the toilets used by your staff are reported to be out of action. Would you:
    a) tell your staff they can use the management toilets at any time? (2 marks)
    b) arrange for your staff to use toilets in an adjacent department? (1 mark)
    c) tell your staff that you are not a plumber and they will just have to wait until they get home? (0 marks)

4) Your boss complains about your department's performance and says that most of your staff are useless. Do you:
    a) stoutly defend them? (2 marks)
    b) admit that some of them are below par, but tell him that you have initiated a training programme? (1 mark)
    c) agree with him and proceed to denigrate each individual in turn? (0 marks)

QUESTIONS: Group 2 (1–16 Circumference scale)

5) Machinery/equipment in your department breaks down, bringing work to a halt. Would you:
   a) move heaven and earth to get it repaired/have replacements brought in? (4 marks)
   b) switch your staff to other productive work? (2 marks)
   c) send your staff home and blame everything on the maintenance people? (o marks)

6) It looks as though your organisation might lose a lucrative contract. Would you:
   a) drop everything and go to the customer/client immediately? (4 marks)
   b) telephone the customer/client? (2 marks)
   c) express surprise that your organisation got the contract in the first place, then return to doing the crossword? (o marks)

7) You have planned a long-awaited evening out with your wife and then your boss says that you must attend a meeting. Would you:
   a) tell your wife to forget the evening out, and risk a divorce? (4 marks)
   b) leave the meeting early and salvage some of the evening? (2 marks)
   c) say you cannot make the meeting as you have slipped a disc carrying home computer print-outs? (o marks)

8) When desperately needed supplies arrive they are found to be wrongly delivered. Do you:
   a) demand an immediate delivery of correct material? (4 marks)
   b) try and adapt the faulty materials for use? (2 marks)
   c) blame it all on one of your staff and then take the rest of the day off? (o marks)

These scores from Group 1 and Group 2 questions are respectively plotted up the 1–8 Radius scale and around the relevant Circumference of the target below. A line is then drawn round the perimeter of the area covered.

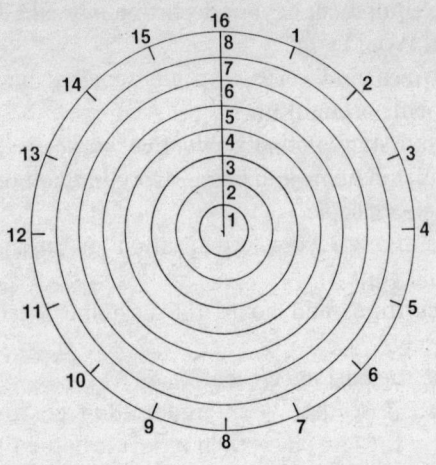

Score	Style
0–0	fox
8–0	goat
8–16	snake
0–16	tiger

There are many management techniques that you will have to master before you can become a fully fledged fox and score a bulls-eye on the Survival Quotient. Of course, you are not alone in this quest and there may well be others in your organisation who have already achieved this coveted status and who might be willing to give you a few tips to help you along.

But how do you find such a paragon? There are certain tell-tale signs that you must look for, although you must be careful not to broadcast your discovery of them or you will have made an enemy for life. These are:

- his boss thinks well of him and comments on the man's ver-satility
- he comes every day to work with a large briefcase which con-tains only his sandwiches, a newspaper and a fat novel (for reading at lunchtime, he says!)

46

- his desk is always clear
- he always knows where the boss is, where he has been and where he is going
- he seldom writes memos
- he regularly takes the minutes at more than one type of meeting
- customers/clients are not sure of his name or title, very few of them have ever talked to him on the phone and none of them have ever met him

If you discover a manager in your organisation with these attributes, make friends with him fast because he is worth his weight in gold to you.

When your Survival Quotient is at 1.00 and your target area covers only the bulls-eye, you will have achieved complete foxhood and qualified as a first-class survivalist in the corporate jungle.

ESSENTIAL SKILLS

Being a fox in management is essentially a minimalist role – that is, you must appear to do enough to retain your credibility as a manager while not over-taxing yourself, bearing in mind at all times that you did not want the job in the first place. In any case, you know that extra effort on your part would go unrecognised. So far, there has been no recorded case of a manager achieving the ultimate goal of being able to stay at home and having his salary sent round once a month, although most organisations have at least one executive who comes near to this desirable state. (Of course, such an achievement must never be recognised, as the very essence of managerial foxhood is to be a fox without being identified as such!)

There are a number of skills and qualities which, we are told, are essential to someone who wishes to be successful in management. Leaving aside the management theorists' more fanciful and capricious notions (in some cases this leaves us with very little!), these are generally thought to be:

- leadership
- the effective use of authority
- the ability to motivate staff
- the ability to exercise discipline

(these are sometimes collectively referred to as 'interpersonal skills' by educated people who ought to know better and by uneducated people who don't)

- the ability to make decisions
- the willingness to accept responsibility

The implication is that if you do not have all or most of these skills and qualities, you cannot be an effective manager. This is based on a false premise, not to say hokum, and derives from a phenomenon known as 'creative structurality'. In order to have any management theories to expound, the management guru must create some; a structure must be given to that which is inherently unstructured. He must define it and describe it before he can posit it. Contrary to popular belief, few if any of these are 'pet' theories, as the guru is smart enough to know that today's meat is tomorrow's poison: this year's theory, which will once and for all solve all management problems at a stroke, will next year be gathering dust alongside books and papers on decentralisation, management by objectives and one minute managing. However, it keeps the theorists in a manner to which they should not be accustomed.

LEADERSHIP

This is the much-vaunted quality prized above all others in management, the magic catalyst which turns base men into golden boys. Simply find yourself a good leader and the lacklustre performance of disinterested workers will be magically transformed into record-breaking achievements in higher output, decreased costs and improved quality. This all sounds fine and plausible, but it is too easy an answer by half. Leadership implies that you go out in front and do what has to be done, so that those whom you are leading not only know where to go, but what to do when they get there. The trouble with being out in front and doing things first is that:

- you are highly visible and so are all your mistakes
- you cannot see what anyone else is doing
- you are liable to attack from behind by your own staff and from the flanks by your colleagues
- you are liable to arrive at your destination only to find that your staff have never left base camp

No, leadership and management are incompatible. If you want to be a dead hero, be a leader; if you wish to be a survivor, stay at the rear and issue orders. After all, how many generals or kings do you see nowadays rushing across the battlefield shouting 'Follow me, men'? Do they say 'Lead in the marines'? Of course not; they say 'Send in the marines'. And why? Because they have learned their lesson. A considerable number of royalty and assorted generals fell at the front before one king, who wished to remain anonymous, declared 'Sod this for a game of soldiers', and promptly stopped to tie his shoelace so that his men might overtake him. What they don't teach you in Harvard Business School is what every manager should learn to recognise instinctively: when to stop and tie your shoelace.

'That man is a born leader', they say. Well, nobody's perfect and given time he may grow out of it. The problem today is that those considered not to be born leaders are likely to be bundled off on a leadership course by some fanatical training manager. Apart from pleading lack of time due to overwork there is not much you can do except attend the course, participate and make all the right noises, whilst closing your ears to the false doctrine. You can then return to work refreshed and carry on much as before. Never be reticent about sending someone else on a leadership course, because in common with all other training courses that is what they are for: other people.

How often does your boss come down among your staff, roll up his sleeves, then show them what to do and exhort them to greater efforts? Often? Not a bit of it. He says to you, 'Here. This is what I want done. Get on with it,' then returns to more serious management matters such as finding out why his secretary has not yet brought his coffee (no doubt because she's on the 'phone being told who did what to whom and when!), or checking with his car dealer why it is taking so long to fit a quadrophonic sound system to the new car, and anyway wasn't that supposed to be standard equipment on the new Super DeLuxe GT model? But, however annoying it may appear to you at the time, the technique your boss has just used on you is one of the magic elements of successful management. Goodbye leadership; let's give a big hand to delegation.

DELEGATION

The trouble with management is that most people forget what it is supposed to be. The better to illustrate this, let us first take a look at what it is not:

- rolling up your sleeves and getting stuck in beside your staff
- patiently sitting for hours trying to explain to your people why you want them to do what you have asked
- 'meeting the needs' of each individual (that's a job for a psychiatrist, not a manager)
- wasting valuable time on crack-brained schemes such as 'job enrichment', 'work structuring' or 'environmental incentives'
- having staff 'participate' in management decisions (curiously, this is known as 'industrial democracy' when in fact the results are more akin to anarchy. Do you know any politicians that would give the electorate that kind of power on every decision?). If your staff start any of that nonsense, just ask them, on the 'If you're so smart, why ain't you rich?' principle, why they are staff and not managers

The plain truth is that over the years the concept of management has become encrusted with all kinds of irrelevancies, which have distorted the simplicity of its form. The job of a manager, in any and every position, is simply to decide what has to be done and then ensure that it gets done. He is not there actually to do anything himself: and that is where delegation comes in.

The key to effective delegation, and therefore to trouble-free management, is to pick the correct people to whom you will delegate each and every task which has to be carried out. And the cardinal rule here is: don't pick the brightest and most able candidates, because this will only spell trouble for you sooner or later. You are the manager and you don't want a bunch of pushy know-alls pestering you with smart ideas every five minutes, otherwise before you know it they will be trying to take your job over. If they are too capable they will be able to do their jobs with relative ease and will then have time to get involved in corporate politics. This would be disastrous, as they would then be able to obtain the same information as you. In your department you do have the monopoly on corporate politics, so pick a bunch of plodders who are malleable and barely competent. This will prove beneficial to you in a number of ways:

- they will be so surprised and grateful at their promotion that they will slave away unceasingly, which is just as well, because you are going to load them with work
- they will pose no threat to your managerial status
- having seen the low calibre of person able to get promotion, their staff in turn will work all the harder, under the mis-apprehension that they too will no doubt be promoted
- you will have distinct advantage over your peers in the organ-isation as they will have much less time for real management (e.g. politics, intrigue, rumour-mongering, etc), since they will be fighting off not only their bosses' unwelcome attentions, but also those of their able and pushy staff

Indeed, if properly handled in this way your staff should be coming to you and begging for more work. This phenomenon and the reasons behind it have recently come to light after a research programme carried out in organisations of all types across the country by a group of behavioural psychologists. According to their research, 'This is a form of masochism which seems to thrive in the corporate climate.' It has been given the working name of 'The HMA (Hit Me Again) Syndrome', and appears to arise in the following way. It is a well known fact that all members of an organisation (except MBAs) expect to be hard done by and put upon, that their lives at work will generally be miserable, without enjoyment or satisfaction, and with constant aggravation from one quarter or another. Managers, too, do not expect to have an easy time, sit with their feet up, take novels in to stave off boredom, etc., and would fail to recognise any of these as a 'work situation'. It therefore follows that the more work individuals have to do, and the more failure and frustration they experience, the better they like it, because this proves to them that they are doing the accepted thing, which accords with their perceived view of work. As a consequence they will continually seek more painful experiences such as having impossible tasks thrust upon them, in the belief that this is a sure way to prove their worth to the organisation.

Of course, this masochism is a heaven-sent opportunity for the manager intent on total delegation and it should be exploited to the full. Moreover, an additional bonus for the highly accomplished manager is that his staff will view his relaxed approach to work as a major error and strive even harder to merit replacing him after his imminent and inevitable downfall.

As long as they are divided up equally, it is of little importance which tasks you delegate to which subordinates; after all, you would not wish to be unfair. If you frequently switch the tasks and the staff for which your subordinates are responsible you will keep everyone on their toes, as they will just be getting used to their new positions when it will be all change again. This is known as the 'Ministerial Method' of management, after the political practice of frequent move-ment of government ministers from department to department, so that we can have a Minister of Agriculture who doesn't know a bull from a bucket, and an Energy minister with a distinct lack of it. In this way no-one has time to become complacent about his job or prove a challenge to the premier.

Do not believe anything that you read about not being able to delegate responsibility or accountability. When you delegate, go all the way. Responsibility, accountability, or any other old thing you care to throw in, because there are no half measures in management. You will find that people do respond to authority, indeed they expect it, so when you tell them, 'Listen, from now on you do all the work and I do all the watching,' they will be grateful for this clear guidance. Your staff have a right to know where they stand, and years later they will come back and thank you. It is times like these which give some of the greatest satisfaction in management and make the job seem almost worthwhile.

MOTIVATION
In motivating people it does not matter what method you use as long as it works. Of course, the same method will not work with everyone and you must therefore have a number of techniques available to ensure success with each individual. Some of the more commonplace methods are set out below.

Money

This is perhaps the most widely used and effective motivator, contrary to the theories of Messrs Maslow and McGregor, who would apparently have us believe that people only pick up their salaries in order to stop their employers worrying about what else to do with the money. Forget about a hierarchy of needs, hygiene factors and so forth – just mention overtime working at time-and-a-half or bonuses for good work, then wait for the rush.

Promises

These are the most versatile because, as you have no intention of fulfilling them, you can be as imaginative and magnanimous as you like! The reward, such as promotion, must be dependent upon some kind of achievement, but an unspecified one, e.g. 'If you work hard enough, I can promise you that promotion will not be too far off.' This is specific enough to motivate (note the use of the word 'promise'), but so vague ('work hard enough' and 'not be too far off') that no claim of achievement could so much as be entertained. You naturally assure the person that he is working well, and that with just a little bit of extra effort he will make the grade. When, if ever, he is judged to have achieved it is up to you ... If anyone ever does make such a superhuman effort that his claim is irrefutable, you can simply say that your boss has put a block on all staff movement and additional expenditure; if it was up to you you would be lashing out pay rises and promotions like there was no tomorrow, but there is nothing you can do. After a few weeks, you tell the individual, 'I've noticed that your performance has fallen off recently. Unless it improves drastically, I can promise you that demotion will not be too far off.'

Competition

One of the most effective ways to get the most out of your staff is through competition. This can be encouraged between individuals, departments or different companies within a group. While departmental or company-wide competition can produce good results, there is no doubt on a personal level that rivalry between staff members fires them with such enthusiasm to come out on top that they will trample anyone who gets in their way; tasks which were previously considered difficult, if not impossible, will be carried out with consummate ease, long working hours will be embraced as a saviour of sanity, and innovative ideas will be generated and implemented with amazing frequency. As in all aspects of man management, the key to this technique is to have your staff self-motivated – the human equivalent of the yet-to-be-discovered perpetual motion engine.

There are a number of ways to achieve this desirable state. For example:

- by spreading the rumour that there may shortly have to be some pruning of staff
- by letting it be known that a quality office will soon be vacant (often the same effect can be achieved by the use of much simpler things such as a rubber plant or a glass-fronted bookcase)
- by starting some cheap competition such as 'Manager of the Month', with a really useful and prestigious prize such as the use of the Chairman's Rolls-Royce for a week (despite the fact that you as a fox would never wish to participate in such a competition, far less run the risk of winning it!)
- by telling selected staff that someone will shortly be required to undertake a business trip to some exotic foreign location

When all else fails you can make an appeal to your staff's better nature. This must only be used as a last resort as you cannot afford to let your staff believe that you have gone soft enough to think that anyone has a better nature. Try taking one of your staff aside and telling him in the strictest confidence that you are in the boss's bad books because your performance has been falling off badly, giving one of the following reasons:

- you have had to sit up nights with a sick mother/spouse/child and then come to work dog tired
- the boss has been complaining about your staff for some time, but due to their good behaviour in the past, you have been reluctant to pass on the reprimands
- you have a chance of promotion, if your department turns in a good performance (this is especially effective if you are unpopular with your staff)

DECISION-MAKING

Over the years there has been much written about the subject of decision-making in management, most of which has been hogwash. Managers have been urged to carry out break-even analyses, cost-benefit analyses, market surveys, samplings and similar mysterious techniques before coming to a decision, but to what end? Despite all this fancy number-crunching and pseudo-scientific nonsense, about eight out of ten new products still fail in the marketplace and about forty per cent of managerial decisons prove to be wrong, sometimes disastrously so. The use of these evaluation methods in no way improves the hit rate, it merely serves to reassure the decision-taker that he has left no stone unturned. No, there is only one rule in the making of decisions: of the two or three which come to mind when you are faced with a problem, always take the first one. Your success rate over all will never be much more than about fifty or sixty per cent in any event, so why waste time agonising over each possible course of action? Much better to leave it to chance. Besides, the speed and decisiveness which will be apparent in using this method will impress your boss and your staff, thereby mitigating your failure rate.

If the course of action you have chosen to take is obvious, has no possible pitfalls and is likely to be popular, take it yourself; if it has no more than two of these attributes, dump it onto someone else by:

- telling one of your staff that it's about time he got some practice if he's ever going to get anywhere
- being absent at the crucial time, so that your boss or one of your staff has to make the decision
- making the decision yourself then telling a staff member to execute it. Write a memo instructing him to do the opposite, but don't send him a copy. If the decision turns out to be a good one, destroy the memo; if it is wrong, blame the staff member and show him the memo. Is anyone going to believe that he conveniently didn't get a copy?

Never put off making a decision because 'something better might turn up soon'. The only thing likely to turn up is your boss, wanting to know why you have not made a decision! As we know, the essence of decision-making is swiftness and sureness; don't worry if you are going swiftly and surely in the wrong direction. Remember, it is style that counts, and anyway, by the time someone has formed the opinion that you may have taken the wrong decision, circumstances will almost certainly have changed and invalidated most of the original considerations.

THE ESSENCE OF MANAGEMENT

Managers are busy people; that is, busy involving themselves in corporate politics, rumour-mongering, laying traps for unwary colleagues and keeping an ear to the ground. They do not have time to study great tomes on management philosophy and practice or to try to extract a modicum of applicable sense from them (and if they did it would only be to find that it is scarcer than rocking-horse droppings). What the busy manager needs to know is the essence of management, an easily remembered guide that will serve in most situations that he is likely to encounter.

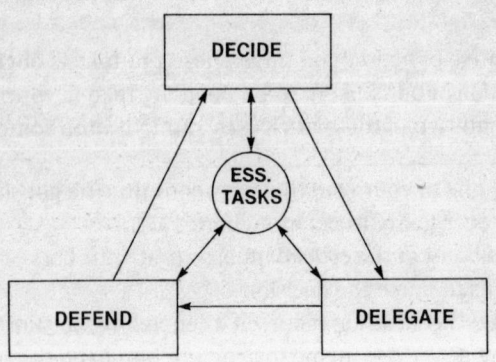

After an exhaustive study of available books, theses and articles, and the conducting of extensive field trials, the '3-D Management Framework' has been constructed by a Swedish management consultant. This framework gives a dimensionality to the three actions surrounding and supporting the execution of Essential Tasks, actions which are present in every managerial function.

Essential Tasks have been defined by Consultant Spektiv as 'those managerial tasks which must be accomplished in order to ensure that the manager is not discovered to be ineffective'. The three elements in the management framework which must be executed in the correct sequence are:

1) *Decide* what is to be done, who is to do it, in what manner and when it is to be done.
2) *Delegate* the work to the chosen victim, making quite plain the concomitant inducements/sanctions/coercion, etc.
3) *Defend* the decision, regardless of whether the outcome appears to be beneficial or not. No management action or decision is intrinsically good or bad, but is relative to other actions and decisions that could have been taken and would almost certainly have produced a worse result (in any case, as you cannot simultaneously apply two different courses of action to the same task, the relative merits of the chosen and the rejected courses of action are unprovable!).

By using the '3-D Management Framework' you can fit any problem or situation to the three stages. Trying to concoct an individual solution for each management problem would take up far too much time and, as previously stated, would not improve your success rate. With the '3-D Management Framework' you will achieve a steadfastness and consistency in your managerial approach which will surprise your friends and astound your enemies. At the same time, you will have learned one of management's basic tenets: keep it simple, and keep it to yourself.

6 COMMUNICATIONS

'Tell a man once, tell a man twice, third time ... tell the new man.'

Joseph Stalin

One of the commonest causes of inefficiency in organisations is the inability of management and staff to communicate, between one department and another or even between individual executives. As with every other aspect of bureaucracy, communication has to be managed, not to say manipulated, if it is to convey the correct message to its intended destination. If you are to be a manager worth his salt, a trainee fox and a survivor, you must learn the art of communication with all possible haste. Your continuing existence within the organisation will depend on it. If you do not learn the verbal skills and epistolary techniques in a fairly short time, you might well be the best manager in the world (which is unlikely, given that you did not want the job in the first place), but you could still end up in a job queue, having been out-communicated by the roar of the tigers and the bleating of the goats.

Many organisations overtly support the principle that communication should be simply a matter of conveying facts, decisions and opinions to all relevant parties as lucidly and speedily as possible: to know is to understand, to understand is to support. But what might be all right for management books or Grimm's fairy tales won't save you amongst the traps and trip-wires of the corporate jungle. Like the Man in the Iron Mask, the truth is shut away for fear of discovery, and an acceptable version is constructed for popular or individual consumption. Perception is all: the truth should have as little bearing as possible on the practice of management, whether it concerns sales figures, efficiency ratios, executive expenses or assurances given to trade unions. On the occasions where 'truth' is required, it can come in various shapes and sizes, depending on who is retailing it. Various examples are set out below.

Facts

These are usually accompanied by some executive assurance such as

- 'You'll just have to take my word for it.'
- 'We've got to lay our cards on the table here.'
- 'Have I ever lied to you before?'
- 'Well, the figures are all there if you want to plough through them yourselves.'

Facts need only have a nodding acquaintance with the truth, but they must have a sufficient amount of credibility to be swallowed by the unsuspecting recipient.

Half-truths

These occur when telling part of the truth is of advantage to the teller, while the other part is generally suppressed by 'facts' (half-truths are especially useful where the veracity of the first part can be demonstrated, thereby encouraging the recipient to assume that the second part is equally truthful). Generally a half-truth would be preceded by some such platitude as:

- 'The truth of the matter is ...'
- 'Strictly between you and I ...'
- 'There's no point in sticking our heads in the sand on this one.'

In some instances the avoidance of revealing the truth has been inculcated into management to such an extent that, even when the truth would be more conducive to the achievement of corporate goals, it is not revealed. This 'tactical faction' is perfectly acceptable when it is used to sustain corporate credibility. After all, there is no intention of concealing the facts in the long term. Luckily, the long term can be as long as you choose to make it.

The Truth

The truth, the whole truth and nothing but the truth, must be avoided at almost any cost, as it generally leads only to making a situation awkward, embarrassing or difficult to handle, and besides, people may come to expect it on a regular basis. Of course, there may be times when telling the truth is absolutely unavoidable, such as when the bailiffs are carrying the organisation's office equipment out the front door, or your biggest customer has just burst into your boss's office hot foot from his idle factory and with your name on his lips. Apart from such unfortunate occasions, well-constructed 'faction' is better for everybody, because it has been designed specifically for the recipients, and we all know that 'made-to-measure' is better than 'off-the-peg' every time. The trouble with the straight truth is that it is so unmalleable – it can't be managed.

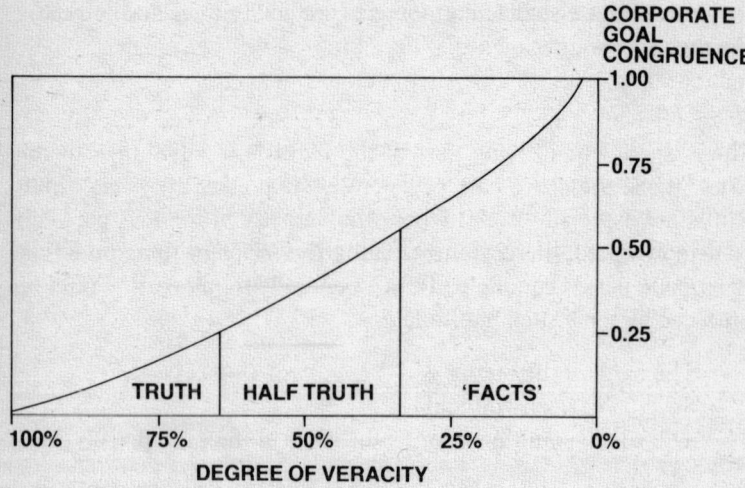

Now that we have established the nature of the information which is to be communicated, let us review the methods available to the manager. These can be of three main types: verbal, written or visual, of which the first two are far and away the most common within organisations. There are of course other means of communication, for example aural, which are much less in evidence. One such example could take the form of the strangled cry of the chief executive as he glances over the latest sales figures, or the rifle-crack of his knuckles as he sees the plunging line on the production graph which you have just placed on his desk from the doorway with the aid of a long pole. But for practical purposes these methods can be ignored as being largely involuntary and therefore unmanageable. Your job must be to learn the primary skills and techniques in verbal and written communications.

VERBAL COMMUNICATIONS

However verbal communication takes place, whether by telephone, informally, at a meeting or conference, it is of considerable benefit if you have developed a strong, commanding and above all self-assured manner of speech. In this way, without actually wanting to become one, you will take on the natural sound and aura of a born leader; you should practise this voice by standing in the middle of a room, adopting an upright posture, arms akimbo, chin jutting aggressively and repeating loudly and clearly such phrases as 'Now listen to me, Sonny Jim, and I'll tell you what the real facts are', 'I have already studied this subject exhaustively', and 'What we need here is a consensus and therefore I have decided that . . .'. After practising this approach on newsvendors, cab-drivers and the like you will soon get the hang of it and become recognised as being naturally superior and a manager of no little distinction. By acting as though you were a born leader you will soon take on the appearance of actually being one.

THE TELEPHONE

Although many people curse this device it is in fact a vital piece of equipment in the modern manager's armoury. Not only can you quickly reach numerous people in many locations without moving from your desk (constant movement is always a bad sign in a manager); you can also, in a steady and reassuring tone, understate, exaggerate or lie with impunity, safe in the knowledge that you will go undetected. (It must be borne in mind that when you enter management you leave all standards of truthfulness, decency and fair play behind. You are in a company now, not a convent.) You should therefore attempt to use the telephone whenever possible, at least until you have moved into the upper echelons of management when you will have mastered the skill of acting simultaneously with your voice, face and body. This behaviour is generally known as the Method School of Management or the Stanislavsky School.

As the telephone is especially useful in situations where information of dubious veracity has to be given to the listener, it can be used most effectively for:

- assuring a customer that his goods should be arriving with him at any moment, when in fact they have not even been despatched from your premises
- quickly spreading rumours round your organisation
- pretending that you are someone else and diverting a call from an irate customer/client to one of your colleagues
- mimicking one colleague's voice and giving false information to another
- pretending to be a customer/client and complaining bitterly to your managing director about the attitude and/or performance of a manager you wish to do down

These are only some of the numerous ways of using the telephone to your advantage, and time spent devising new methods will be repaid tenfold in terms of strategic advantage and the downfall of your corporate enemies.

DICTATING MACHINES

These are excellent for spreading rumours or laying false trails (they are also very good for privately conveying messages of a more personal kind). At the end of your dictated letter or report, record the information you wish to be conveyed as though it has been partly recorded over and left on the tape in error. Within minutes of its discovery, every detail will be all round the organisation. The information could take the form of:

- a letter of application for another job, due to lack of promotion/inadequate salary in the present one
- a letter of reply defending your boss against outrageous allegations of incompetence made against him by one of your colleagues
- part of a note advising another manager to break off his affair with the chief executive's wife, and how could he do such a thing while still awaiting the results of the pregnancy test on the Purchasing Director's daughter?

Be as brutal as you like; remember, this is a struggle for survival and there's no room for sentiment. You can always assure your colleague at his leaving party that you'll do your best to find the rat who put the boot into him (in this example, remember not to use your own dictating machine!).

DISCUSSIONS, MEETINGS, ETC

By far the most common means of verbal communication is face-to-face discussion with one or more persons. An arrogant approach and the commanding voice you have been practising will be invaluable here. For instance, when conducting a disciplinary interview with one of your staff, do not be afraid to browbeat him or to use emotional blackmail. Make it clear that what you are about to say is for his ears only and that if he repeats it you will deny every word ... then lay into him with a will:

- 'Is this any way to act after all I've done for you?'
- 'You've not only let me down but you've let yourself and your family down as well.'
- 'I've seen a lot of mean actions in my time, but this beats them all.'

If this sounds a little harsh on a man merely for being three minutes late for work, you must bear in mind that discipline should be in evidence at all times, otherwise you could have a revolt on your hands. This is especially important when you first join an organisation, as in the early stages people will be testing your mettle.

Of course, the browbeating approach may not work with everyone. It is important to have in your verbal repertoire such techniques as:

- a low, sycophantic tone, which is a verbal version of crawling on all fours, for addressing corporate executives
- an affable 'I'm one of the boys' tone, for use with colleagues and with your staff when you wish to gain their confidence and allay suspicion that you are on the side of the boss
- an avuncular 'How can I help you' tone, for use with chronic complainers and trade union representatives
- an aggressive 'I'll come round there and sort you out' tone, for dealing with clients/customers who expect that you've got nothing better to do than run after them all day

Other verbal communication techniques which can be useful are:

- deliberately misunderstanding someone and looking at him as though he had lost his marbles
- if the speaker has a strong accent, continually saying 'Pardon? I can't understand you. It must be your accent.' After a short time he will get embarrassed and simply go away
- saying, 'I find it very difficult to understand you. Do you realise that your dentures don't move when you're talking?'
- in the middle of someone making an important point, saying, 'Excuse me staring, but has your nose always been that way?'

On the other hand, when talking to a group of people, perhaps your departmental workforce, the techniques you should use are somewhat different. First of all, arrange the meeting to commence no more than ten or fifteen minutes before the lunch-break or finishing time. In this way you will ensure that the meeting will be short and sweet. You might even consider using the old trade union tactic of announcing a members' meeting in one location then switching it to another and only telling selected members, thereby ensuring a unanimous vote for a controversial measure. At your meeting you must adopt the commanding stance and tone of voice which you have been practising, telling your listeners that you will take any questions at the end of the meeting. If anyone is so bold as to interrupt with a question, stare at him then look around at his colleagues in a bewildered fashion. After a suitable pause, ask the offending questioner, 'What on earth has that got to do with it? Don't you understand anything of what I've been standing here telling you for the last ten minutes?' (No matter if it has only been three minutes; he won't have been timing you!)

FORMAL MEETINGS, COMMITTEES, ETC.

It is a well-known fact that the greater the number of management meetings held in an organisation, the greater is its efficiency. It is of little consequence whether these gatherings are called Management Meetings, Budget Meetings, Steering Committees – a title which implies that its members exhibit some sense of direction! – or any one of a multitude of titles. In some organisations the situation develops into 'management by meeting', where the unfortunate participants migrate from one room to another, from a Budget Sub-committee Meeting via a Safety Meeting to a Computer Implementation Steering Committee like a bedraggled camel caravan, laden with files, minutes and memos, bleary-eyed from the smoke, bloated with coffee and perhaps even dragging their chairs with them. All in the name of good management.

Never make the mistake of thinking that these meetings are for making decisions: far from it. Their primary function is to provide each participant with a chance to parade his skill, knowledge and efficiency before those around the table, and at the same time to expose, embarrass and denigrate his fellow managers. However spurious the supposed purposes of meetings are, you must recognise that they are of paramount importance in management: each one is a set-piece, a stage on which you can shine or shrivel, a battlefield where you can win your colours or retire defeated. As this is such a highly competitive environment, in true fox fashion you must contrive to weight the odds in your favour before it gets down to hand-to-hand fighting in the trenches. According to the composition of the committees/meetings, there are a number of ways of going about this, e.g.

- few people relish the task of taking the minutes at a meeting as they believe it restricts their ability to participate. They fail to recognise the considerable influence wielded by the minute-taker if he handles the task correctly. If you can manage to get this job at one or more meetings you will have gained a major advantage over your colleagues, because you will then decide what goes into the minutes, and more importantly, what does not. This is especially important if non-attending senior management receive copies of the minutes. Having been appointed minute secretary you must quickly develop a reputation for being consistently late with the minutes. Not too late, but just enough to ensure that the participants do not remember with any accuracy what was said at the meeting. Given these conditions, the rest is up to you
- changing the agenda of a meeting at the last minute and not giving a copy to a rival
- if a contentious subject is due to be brought up at a meeting,

spend some time writing a memo which clearly and strongly puts your point of view and the associated benefits, then, about ten minutes before the meeting commences, distribute copies to the participants. They will have time to read your memo but not to formulate a reasoned reply and you will have gained a distinct advantage over them

- always have plenty of evidence/data to hand which you can withdraw from a folder with a flourish at a critical moment to surprise and confound your enemies. Of course, this data need not be strictly correct, as long as nobody else is allowed to get their hands on it. As in all verbal encounters, you should appear completely confident in what you are saying, by quoting dates, precise quantities, exact locations, etc. If necessary, make up these details: there is always room for greater creativity in modern management. In this way you can catch your rivals on the wrong foot, as they are unlikely to have dossiers to match yours

- this method of undermining a rival is particularly effective if his boss is also at the meeting. At the earliest possible point in the proceedings, when you have everyone's attention, jokingly enquire of the victim as to the truth of a rumour that he has made a major blunder in some aspect of his work which he has tried to keep quiet. Of course he will deny it, and then you will say, 'I didn't believe it for a minute, but you'd wonder at people starting rumours like that for no reason at all.' After that his effectiveness at the meeting will be nil, as he cowers before the gimlet eyes of his boss!

The strategy and tactics needed for meetings and the preparation for them is a subject on its own, and is worthy of considerable study. However, there is one golden rule which must be adhered to at all times: never go into a meeting without knowing what to expect from the other participants and being well prepared to deal with it. Although they may naïvely believe that they are there to discuss departmental and corporate goals and to make decisions, you know better.

WRITTEN COMMUNICATIONS

The principal point to be remembered about written communications is that they are a permanent record of what is being communicated so you must only use them when absolutely necessary; you do not want to go offering any hostages to fortune. Let other people commit themselves on paper to you if they must: it can be a valuable source of information at a later date and for this reason you should never throw out any letters, telexes, memos or the like, unless they incriminate you or would tend to show retrospectively that your judgement had been wrong.

In order that the material you have collected remains for your eyes only, ensure that no-one else possesses a key to your desk or filing cabinet. If you receive a new desk, make sure that you get both sets of keys. At some point you may suspect that someone may be having a look through your files. If so, wet both ends of a hair and stick it across a drawer or door opening then check to see if it is there the next day. Even better, plant false information in a prominent place then sit back and watch the fun! All of this may sound dramatic but it is essential to protect yourself in the competitive atmosphere of many organisations. Given the opportunity in the relentless quest for useful information, many managers are not averse to having a quick rifle through a colleague's files. You can be sure that at least one of the long-serving managers has keys which will fit just about every desk, cupboard and filing cabinet in the organisation. A key stamped 'master' on anyone's key-ring is a dead giveaway.

In this context, the person who has to be watched is the one who consistently carries on working after everyone else has gone home. There can only be four possible reasons for this kind of aberrant behaviour:

- he is trying to impress the boss. But, as anyone smart enough to become the boss is unlikely to be at work after hours, the late worker will have to inform his superior about his sterling work. In such a case he may just as well say that he is working late then leave shortly after everyone else has gone home
- he is incompetent and cannot finish his work within normal working hours

- given the choice of working late or going home to his wife he chooses working late as the lesser of two evils
- he is raking through the files of other managers

While this latter type of underhand action may be condemned in a colleague who was a trusted friend and confidante, there is nothing to stop you doing it, as you are certainly not bound by the same set of standards as those which apply to other members of your organisation – if you were, you would be a goat and not a fox.

Where written communications are concerned it is not important whether you are competent in spelling, grammar and punctuation, as recent surveys have shown that many people have reached senior managerial positions without being able to express themselves in anything more than kindergarten English. You will undoubtedly have come across a colleague of the 'How many zeds in resignation?' type. Excessive competence in this field could in fact prove to be a definite drawback as you will probably be accused of being an intellectual, a pedant, or having copied out of a book. Nevertheless, some knowledge as to the form and content of letters and memos is needed so that they can at least be effective (if not masterpieces of literary art)

LETTER WRITING

In your capacity as manager there will be times when you cannot avoid writing a letter, however hard you try. It is important on these occasions to use the correct terminology for the person you are addressing, e.g. if you wish to antagonise him, address him by a lesser title than the one he deserves, such as Sales Manager instead of Sales Director. Conversely if you wish to butter him up, make sure you give him a title at least one management level above his own. (It is interesting to note which ones make a point of correcting you and which ones are prepared to let you go on thinking that they are Sales Directors!)

As you will not be writing many letters (it is not possible to write voluminous letters while keeping an ear to the grapevine and both eyes on your future and your fellow competitors), a few standard ones should suffice. Indeed, if you have copies of these made on your company's notepaper you can simply strike out those elements which are not required on each occasion. This will not only save your valuable managerial time but also that of your secretary who can then concentrate on those tasks she thinks essential: spreading rumours, spreading the dirt on colleagues and influencing the boss in your favour. An additional bonus with this procedure is that the recipients of your to-the-point letters will be delighted to receive them, as they will immediately recognise the efficiency of your operation. Here are two examples to get you started.

Letter of complaint to suppliers

'Dear Sirs,

Let's stop beating about the bush. If they ever award a Nobel Prize for incompetence, I'll pay your fare to Stockholm.

At first I said to myself, "These people obviously enjoy a joke.... and they'll come around after they've had their fun."

Well, I'm still waiting, and as I'm planning to reach retirement age within the next thirty-five years, I cannot afford to extend your period of grace any further.

So, I'll tell you what I'm going to do. Unless you come up with the required goods/services/carry out the repairs/within seven working days, I'm going to hit you with a lawyer so fast it'll make your head spin.

Yours sincerely.'

With a little adaptation this letter should cover most eventualities in dealing with customers, clients or suppliers. If you state your position clearly and unequivocally, they'll soon come around.

One area where expertise in letter writing can make things easier for you is that of employee relations. If, having talked with a member of staff, you are still dissatisfied with someone's attitude or performance, send that person a letter, outlining your areas of concern. In this way the employee will know where he stands and you will have the evidence on record.

Given a little time and imagination you can adapt a standard letter or write others which are more fitting to your individual requirements. Always bear in mind that people have a right to expect to know where they stand, whether they are suppliers, customers or employees, and will therefore appreciate a personal letter, which clearly and firmly states the position of management.

One of the last letters which you will be required to write will be your letter of resignation. You can of course give your views to your boss verbally before departing but, in the heat of the moment you might not only be incoherent but may say something inappropriate or actionable, or forget some important point which you have been itching to say for years. By writing a letter of resignation you can not only be more lucid and comprehensive but you can also place your views on record, if necessary sending copies to your boss's superior or the whole Board of Directors.

Letter of resignation

'Dear sir,

I wish to resign my present position (of chief lackey) and leave the organisation at the end of the next calendar month (if I am not successful in obtaining a doctor's certificate for the next few weeks).

I have been offered a (proper) job in a (normal) organisation, at an increased salary (which will allow my family and myself to indulge in luxuries such as eating regularly, buying new clothes and being able to choose which furniture the bailiffs take in lieu of unpaid bills). I look back on my time in the organisation with mixed feelings (*i.e.* in the course of a long career, I have never met such a bunch of incompetents, ably led by yourself).

The division/department in which I work is a (total) shambles, with the majority of staff running around (like headless chickens) neither knowing nor caring what goals they are supposed to reach or how they might reach them. Half of them don't even know what day of the week it is, and if they did know would not have the remotest idea what to do with the information. The other half are a bunch of back-stabbing yes-men (who know as much about management as I do about the life cycle of the South American boll-weevil). Morale is at rock bottom (and this is about three steps above what it deserves to be in such a hick outfit).

Your primary objective seems to be to shut yourself in your office, avoid all problems or conflict and give no help, guidance or direction to (that anarchic rabble you call) your management team (given your level of managerial and technical expertise, I suppose this is hardly surprising – a more weak-willed, indecisive and double-dealing person I have yet to meet, and it is understandable that your nickname is Kipper, *i.e.* two faces and no guts).

If the shareholders had the slightest notion that their money was being poured down the drain by (a bunch of tossers such as) you and your henchmen, hanging would be too good for you. Take care that some public-spirited person does not decide to enlighten them.

It will be with the greatest of pleasure that I will leave this organisation and return to sanity once more.

Yours sincerely.'

You will notice that as you do not wish to be personal and would want to keep the relationship on a business-like footing at all times, in the letter above no mention has been made of the recipient's name. Even though you are leaving the organisation, courtesy costs nothing, and it could stand you in good stead in the future.

7 READY FOR DEVELOPMENT

'I've taught you all I know and you still know nothing.'

Aristotle

Although you may have found yourself a tenable, if not a lucrative, position in management, you cannot simply sit back and relax, secure in the knowledge that you have no more to learn of the black art. Tigers and goats may relax but foxes never do. Shortly after entering a new organisation you will find that you are subjected to the nefarious process known as management development, a fancy name which is now used in preference to the old term of 'training', which was more reminiscent of the whip and the chair than the slide projector and the pointer.

The process of management development is one which you will have to undergo intermittently in your management career, so it is important that you know what delights await you. There is no call for despondency as undergoing development does not mean that you are lacking in vital management skills or that your knowledge is redundant and that you must be re-programmed – rather that the Management Development Manager has a salary, office and expense account which he must justify by eliciting academic squeals of pain from as many managers as possible. This should not come as a surprise to anyone except the naïve goats of the organisation, as it follows that age-old management principle: 'It doesn't matter what you do as long as it's big and loud.'

The underlying assumption of this principle is that nothing beats a try and that the individual will surely come up with a viable scheme or product sooner or later, provided that he is allowed enough attempts (and provided that he has not driven the business into liquidation in the meantime!). As usual, the management gurus have hit the nail right on the thumb.

Of course, you may ask yourself the question, 'If I do not undergo management development, how am I going to learn about such exciting new management ruses as:

- management by walking around (so what's new?)
- skunk works
- theory Z (the only consolation here is that, as they have reached the last letter of the alphabet, perhaps they will stop with the theories)
- corporate culture
- intrapreneuring
- T groups

Indeed, how have you managed to survive this far as a manager without them? Well, probably in the same way as managers survived in the 1950s without (or rather in spite of) Thematic Apperception Tests, in the 1960s without Sensitivity Training, and in the 1970s without Management by Objectives. But do you think that will cut any ice with the Management Development Manager in your organisation? You've guessed it! Already he has drawn up a Training Needs Analysis for you and is halfway through your Personal Development Plan. What is this? An analysis? A plan? This must be serious. Of course it is: his job depends on it.

As with most areas of management (or life), the 'experts' in this area will attempt to blind you with science, hitting you around the ears with such verbal karate as the 'hierarchy of cognitive learning objectives'. The what? This is one with which you should become familiar as there may be a financial reward just for being able to say this phrase, and you will almost certainly get promotion for finding out what it means. If you do find out, discreetly tell the Management Development Manager, who may well reward you by recommending that you never go on a training course. You will come up against many examples of this ego-speak, which is defined as 'the deliberate use of words of which the listener is known to be ignorant, in order to enhance the status of the speaker'.

On your journey in the ghost train of management education you will have horrors leaping out at you such as:

- the apperception-interaction method
- cross-over groups or square root groupings

- gestalt therapy
- Kepner and Tregoe approach

Some of these sound as if they might have come from Masters and Johnson rather than from Blanchard and Johnson. You will need all your foxy cunning to weave your way through this particular thicket, but once you are through, other, greater dangers lie in wait for you.

THE SEMINAR

In common with a conjuror's colourful box of tricks, there are a number of management development geegaws to catch your eye, the most ubiquitous being the training course or seminar. At frequent intervals in your career some bright spark will declare with the gleam of discovery in his eye, 'I've got it! What you need is a training course.' That's when you should head for the door fast, because you know that the last thing you need is to spend one or two weeks incommunicado in some remote location, while back at the company your department is slowly going down the tubes, thanks to your helpful fellow managers. Generally the only good reasons for going on a residential training course or seminar are:

- you are physically or mentally run down
- you are badly in need of sleep
- problems at home have become unbearable
- it is budget or stocktaking time in your organisation
- there is some private but pressing reason as to why you should be out of town for a few days

There will be times when you will not be able to avoid going on a training course because your boss will himself have been indoctrinated by the Management Development Manager; besides, it is a well-known fact that money spent on management training is as good as money in the bank.

If you are forced to undertake such a rash venture, it is important that you do so in the correct frame of mind. You are a fox and a survivor and have no wish to be indoctrinated by those who would have you embark on the trail of achievement and success. You must at all times be on your guard against false doctrine.

What then should you do when faced with a week of such penal servitude? As in all other situations, you should use your fox-like qualities to render the situation as painless and amenable as possible by:

- getting to know the tutors well – some of them may be open to bribery
- taking a plentiful supply of cotton wool and sleeping pills
- making an early claim to a permanent rear seat in the lecture room, preferably one near an exit
- starting a poker school with a number of like-minded colleagues
- attaching yourself to a group of four other delegates. For participative exercises, delegates are generally assigned four to a group. If you manage to be fifth man you can spend your time handing out and collecting papers, marking results on the blackboard, etc., and might even get a gold star for helping the tutor.
- consulting with a colleague who has been on the same course and reading his course notes and handouts. In this way you will be able to go to sleep during lectures yet wake when someone nudges you and answer the lecturer's questions
- starting an argument with each lecturer and inciting your colleagues to acts of dissension. You won't win the argument, but it will certainly use up lecture time

However, be careful which tactics you use as there is often a catch at the end of these courses: the lecturer is required to assess you and make a report to your boss.

With any luck a straight bribe might get you the desired result, but some of these people actually believe they are doing a worthwhile job and do not take too kindly to a little gentle persuasion. If a questionnaire has to be completed, you've got a problem, because while you may be able to describe in detail what constitutes a royal flush or how to mix a Rusty Nail, you will certainly not have learned how to appraise an investment by calculating its Net Present Value. This calls for drastic action; you must volunteer to collect the completed papers then drop them on the floor. Picking out the one completed by the smartest person in the class, you apologise for not filling in your name on your paper then discreetly obliterate his and add yours. By the process of elimination your paper will be taken as his, which is understandably left unsigned due to it being such a pathetic effort! Now, what would you have done if you hadn't been a fox?

In order to give the appearance of value for money (but how does one measure that?), most training courses and seminars will contain one or more of the following techniques.

1) THE LECTURE METHOD

Why the lecture method is so widely used is difficult to say as it is largely ineffective, given that most participants are either talking, dozing, worrying about what's happening back in their departments or wondering when the waitress is going to bring in the coffee. This situation is not helped by the fact that each lecturer usually appears to have been chosen because of some physical peculiarity he has, such as a twitch, a soporific voice, an ability simultaneously to talk and spray the furthermost member of the class, or a paranoic tendency to reach for something well below knee level via his trouser pocket. In an extreme case you may be lucky enough to witness all of these phenomena in one person.

At the very least, the lecturer will have a favourite word or phrase which he will frequently repeat, thereby providing some innocent fun for the course members who will take bets on how often the word or phrase will be repeated in a given time and coincidentally hearten the lecturer no end by their rapt attention to his every word. While these tendencies displayed by the lecturer may well be entertaining, they are hardly conducive to learning, and merely lead to boredom, mirth or despair for a group of managers who did not want to be there in the first place. Besides, it is a well-known fact that student recall of lecture material is only some 40 per cent at the end of the lecture period and drops to 20 per cent within seven days. What use it is to the hapless management student after a month is anybody's guess.

As an added refinement, you may find that at the end of each lecture you are given a handout by the lecturer, a synopsis of his pearls of wisdom for you to peruse in your spare time back in your department. If these do not end up strewing the corridor outside the lecture room, like leaflets for cut-price Sanskrit lessons outside the bus station, then they will almost certainly end up in a heap with all the other lecture notes you have gathered over the years and never read.

2) TELEVISED PRESENTATION

This is a traumatic experience which ranks alongside pushing a trolley round a crowded supermarket as one of the most sadistic forms of torture known to modern man. The method consists of each delegate being asked to prepare and deliver a five minute presentation to the other delegates, using a flip chart or blackboard, each performance being recorded on videotape. After everyone has been recorded, each presentation is played back and criticised by the participants.

This is when the real torture begins. Where has that smooth presentation method gone? (or did you ever have it?) Are those your hands flapping about like semaphore flags, your arm sunk to the elbow in your trousers pocket? And if you had scratched your head that often in school they would have had you looking like Yul Brynner as quickly as it took to get the hair clippers out! Following the old adage that there is no such thing as a problem, only an opportunity (try telling *that* to Richard Nixon): on learning that a video session is imminent, you must immediately claim extensive film experience and volunteer to be the cameraman. In this way you can avoid being called to perform until last, by which time you will have smeared the lens or sabotaged the instrument in some other way. You will also be able to decide on the method of recording each participant. This is your big chance to be adventurous, to take close-ups of that trembling pointer, to zoom onto the hand rattling a pocketful of change, or present the nostrils in full flare as the nervous presenter throws back his head in desperation. Given these conditions, if you cannot make a laughing-stock of most of your fellow managers and at the same time avoid any serious participation yourself, you should hand in your fox badge immediately.

3) EXPERIENTIAL EXERCISE

Those management lecturers of a psychological bent (or bent psycho-logically?), very often employ another little party game on training courses known as an Experiential Exercise, in which delegates are asked to take part in a practical exercise. A common task is the building of some kind of structure with children's play bricks, to a given configuration and within a set time. Points are then awarded to each group according to the degree to which the objectives are achieved. There is no necessity here for the fox to get involved, except to sit back watching and listening as groups of adults fight over who gets to place the next brick on top of the carefully built structure or complain to the tutor that they are not going to play any more if Johnny does not give back the brick which he stole. Watch out for tears and flying fists! In order to be of some assistance, you could try discreetly bumping the table at a crucial point in the construction (i.e. the placing of the penultimate brick), to send the whole folly crashing to the floor. Your managerial colleagues will thank you for this practical assistance as you will have helped them to a greater appreciation of real-life situations.

Success in this type of enterprise does not usually result in any tangible reward being given to the winning group, although sometimes, if the group has been especially well behaved, the tutor will allow them games in class the next day.

4) BUSINESS GAMES

Another common feature of the training course or seminar is the Business Game. Why management should treat this theoretical exercise as any more of a game than the everyday business in their organisations remains something of a mystery. The theory behind such games is that they are a microcosm of an actual or typical situation, compressed in time to encompass one or more business cycles, e.g. budget periods, so that actions, reactions and consequences can all be seen and judged. There is no doubt that when it is announced to management students that they will shortly take part in a business game, the normal classroom lethargy seems to fall away from them immediately as eyes narrow, teeth are bared, the sound of scraping steel is heard and the old competitive, not to say killer, instincts start the fingers twitching. What's this? No need to plan ahead or worry about the costs of reckless decisions? Just like the real thing!

Before the commencement of the game proper the participants are usually split up into groups of four, who are then asked to pick their executive officers. At this point it becomes obvious that managers do not wish to take up the same positions as they do in real life: the sales director wants to put his feet up in a cushy purchasing job, the production man wants an easy time of it in sales. Of course, this may also be because their competence in their real jobs is well known to their colleagues, and after all the object of this game is to come out on top.

If you cannot avoid participating in this type of game then you must simply use the same techniques of foxery and underhand actions as you would back in your own organisation, i.e. falsifying figures, sneaking a look at the opposing teams' efforts, inadvertently wiping the data from your computer if you see that the projections of future performance look bad for your group. With certain types of micro-computer you can wipe all the information belonging to a rival group by accidentally pulling out their plug while attending to your own!

Despite the best efforts of the participants (or perhaps because of them), you will almost certainly find that these theoretical organisations make exactly the same hash of running their business as they do in real life. At the end of the session the lecturer will say with a pained smile as he consigns the evidence of bankrupt companies to the bin, 'Never mind, ladies and gentlemen, it is only a game and it can never precisely reflect the conditions in real life.' What does he know? At the same time most of the group members will be saying to themselves 'I'm glad I don't have to do this every day.'

The training course or seminar is the most widely used method of management development, but there are a number of other techniques to which the manager may be subjected. Along with the training course, many of these tend to be ineffective, but as management training has always been looked on as being intrinsically a 'good thing', over the years the training experts have idled away many a happy hour inventing new ways of torture for their hapless victims. In these enlightened days, when it seems fashionable to bring the theatre into the classroom (or in the case of management students, the circus), there are a variety of techniques which are used by the avant-garde trainer.

ACTION LEARNING

A group of five or six managers are put in a room with the objective of discussing either common or individual problems. Each manager is supposed to offer advice to his colleagues, using his own experience of management, and in turn seek advice from them in areas where his experience is inadequate to deal with a current problem. In today's competitive environment this is akin to putting a bunch of cannibals into an empty room and asking them to prepare a meal. At the very least the result will be chaos (and it could degenerate!) with everyone giving each other bogus and misleading advice or bragging about past achievements, most of these statements having only a nodding acquaintance with the truth.

The managers in such a group are certainly not about to assist their colleagues materially or to divulge any hard-won experience. If you do happen to find yourself sober in such a gathering, all you can do is be honest, open and co-operative, i.e. give them the worst possible advice you can invent, swear that you owe your present success to following those very principles (or prior lack of success to ignoring them), and tell them that you are willing to go along and help them in their departments at any time. Alternatively, you can confess to having a major managerial problem and throw yourself on the mercy of the court. In this way you will demonstrate your managerial weakness and they will then dismiss you as a potential rival in the organisational rat-race. Sometimes even the fox has to play dog, and lie down and roll over, because it is a golden rule that the fox should never be recognised as such, except to another fox. In any event, it is more than likely that the whole Action Learning exercise will be a complete waste of time, as you will hear more lies in one short session than you would at a hypochondriacs' convention.

BEHAVIOUR MODIFICATION

Another nice little number advocated by the management developers is Behaviour Modification. This theory claims that people are most likely to engage in desired behaviour if they are rewarded for doing so, especially if the reward immediately follows the desired behaviour. The correctness and simplicity of this proposition is breathtaking and is probably due to the fact that the technique is as old as the hills.

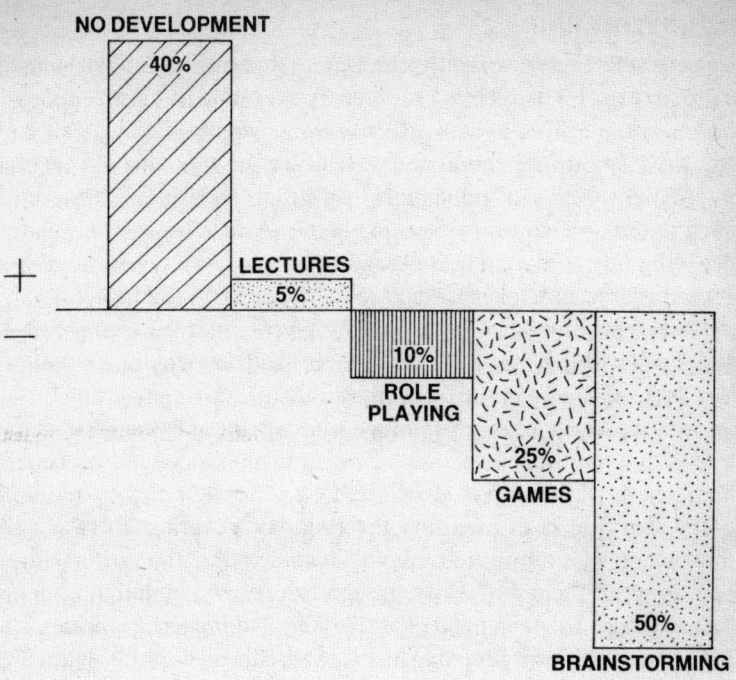

Behaviour modification is the only training method which works with any predictable degree of success, with rewards for managers generally being money and promotion for achievement, or demotion and the sack for failure. People certainly know where they stand with this theory and they are not caught up in any pseudo-scientific calculations in order to determine how well they are doing on the job. The key elements in Behaviour Modification, or Therapy, include reinforcement, conditioning and extinction (greed and fear being the prime motivators), although 'extinction' does seem a little harsh simply for turning in a poor performance. But times are tough in management. In a crude form, Behaviour Modification is widely used by bosses of all types and can be diffiult to counteract. Some methods of doing so are outlined in Chapter Nine.

BRAINSTORMING

Unfortunately this technique presupposes that in any random sample of managers (or sample of random managers), there are enough brains among them to be worth storming. Despite the illogicality of the supposition, the rationale put forward for this idea is that the interactions between individuals in a group can spark off ideas in each other; so if you have nothing better to do, like watching paint dry, why not sit in on a brainstorming session. At the very least you should get enough jokes to keep your friends laughing for weeks.

Managers sitting around a table are given a problem and asked to say the first thing that comes into their heads by way of a solution. You can see the potential already, can't you? Fortunately this is not as arduous a task for many managers as it might at first appear, since this is the way that they make most of their managerial decisions. Someone in the group is given the task of writing down each and every idea that is thrown into the ring, but generally there are so many, and of such mind-numbing banality that the writer either cannot write them down fast enough or cannot stop laughing long enough to get them on paper. For the sake of managerial reputations, in many cases this is probably just as well. The ideas put forward are supposed to be sifted through later and the more extreme ones rejected. But in this context, what is 'extreme'? In any event, the sifting through of ideas rarely takes place with any effectiveness, because either the participants cannot discuss the solutions for rolling about the floor in paroxysms of laughter or the session ends up in a general argument, with each manager vehemently denying that he ever said such a stupid thing.

The most effective way for you to handle any brainstorming session in which you may be forced to participate is to put forward the wackiest ideas you can invent then sit back and listen as the others follow suit, producing solutions so bizarre as to be unbelievable. But do be careful: some of them have been known to be accepted and implemented! With any luck, after one such session, this will be the last you will hear of brainstorming.

Brainstorming is in fact what its name suggests: a temporary seizure of the collective grey matter which results in havoc. While it is not recorded who first came up with the brainstorming idea (probably at a brainstorming session), given the suggestions normally produced it seems likely that Hans Christian Andersen and Edward Lear are two of the front runners.

There are many other management development methods which can trap the unwary survivor, some of which appear under another guise, such as a conference. It is essential that vigilance is exercised at all times, that training and development are recognised for what they are and isolated, so that your head does not get stuffed with all kinds of conformist nonsense. In your chosen role as a survivor, all that you should attempt to develop are your abilities as a fox, and they don't teach you how to do that in Harvard business school, or on management development courses.

8 SEND FOR THE EXPERTS

'An expert is a person who knows more and more about less and less until he knows everything about nothing.'

Marx

Whenever a problem arises for which you do not have an instant answer, there will always be some goat who will bleat, 'Send for the experts. They'll sort it out for you.' If you believe that you'll believe anything. The last thing you need is some so-called expert poking around your department, upsetting your staff and generally disrupting the calm atmosphere you have worked so hard to achieve, for, like any foreign body, the expert is bound to cause irritation. You are the manager, a fox and a survivor, and not only are you quite capable of handling your own problems, but you are equally adept at covering them up or putting the blame for them on somebody else, if necessary.

Unfortunately, though, there are a thousand and one experts near at hand, all of them ready and willing to criticise, pontificate, direct and advise you, to such an extent that you might well think they actually knew something about management. Of course, they may well know something of their own particular trade or profession (though don't bank on it!); what they don't know about is your department and the kind of mediocre, lumpen staff, antedeluvian equipment and autocratic boss with which you must contend. Despite the numerous categories of expert, they all have one thing in common: whenever you don't want them, there they are, dogging your footsteps, and on the very rare ocassion that you could use some help with a major problem, they are nowhere to be seen (while he can in no way be classed as an expert, your boss will often exhibit the same traits).

There are two types of expert; the amateur and the professional, the only distinction being that the former claims expertise in virtually all subjects while the latter generally restricts himself to one.

THE AMATEUR

Within any organisation it is relatively easy to recognise the amateur expert – let's call him Harry – as he will almost certainly betray one or more of the following characteristics:

- he will have at least half a dozen pens marshalled across his breast pocket, accompanied by a small ruler, a pen torch and possibly a tyre pressure gauge
- he will carry about his person enough devices to stock a small tool store, e.g. a selection of screwdrivers in a plastic wallet, a 500-blade penknife, a set of keys which will fit any lock ever invented, a pair of pliers, a tape measure and a small first-aid kit which includes a pair of folding crutches (depending on the state of the politics within the organisation, the first-aid kit may also contain knee plasters and crotch slings)
- in his car he will have a toolkit which would rival that in the engine room of a transatlantic liner
- he constantly works on his car in his spare time, fitting a turbocharger, a special exhaust system and an octophonic sound system (designed by himself). Despite this his car constantly gives him trouble and any lunch break he can be found with his head under the bonnet fiddling with the engine
- he frequently and at length tells you about all the marvellous projects he is carrying out at home, such as adding a new wing or digging an underground fallout shelter with power to be supplied by gas from his compost heap, none of which projects he ever finishes
- he reads avidly every technical magazine from Electronics Digest to Woodwork News
- he is a poor performer in his job

How did Harry become an expert? Simply by telling everyone so often and at such length that he was, that they eventually all gave in and believed him. Public opinion notwithstanding, you should not allow him within a mile of your department if you can avoid it. And yet, if your department is having just a hint of trouble with a photocopier, typewriter, computer or anything of a mechanical, electrical or electronic nature, Harry will appear as though summoned by telepathy.

In he'll stride, chest stuck out, pens gleaming like a row of campaign medals. As he saunters around the offending piece of equipment he gives a little smile and says in an avuncular tone, 'What seems to be the problem, then?' (Notice here that, as you are not an expert like Harry, you can only be expected to say what the problem seems to be.) If he adopts an overly familiar tone and refers to the machine as 'she', you can be sure he has dallied with 'her' before.

Although the Harrys of this world are extremely difficult to dissuade from acts of applied expertise, it is certainly worthwhile making an attempt at this point, before he actually lays hands on anything. There are a number of possibilities here including:

- telling him that the reverse camber spigot balance has broken. As he will not know what this means (you have just made it up), he will probably claim that it is a sealed unit and must be replaced by the service agents
- letting him know that you are having a new one delivered that day, so any work on the old one would be pointless
- informing him that the machine will still work better broken that it will after he has tried to fix it
- felling him with a head-butt or a knee in the groin, although caution is needed here, as he may take offence

Despite these approaches you may find that it is not easy to get rid of your resident expert, as there is no problem too difficult for him to solve, no technology out of his grasp; quantum mechanics and nuclear physics are meat and drink to the man. Before you know it he will have taken off his jacket and laid out his tools on the floor. Machine covers and panels will be removed in a trice and his eyes will gleam at the levers, gears and circuitry laid bare before him. By this time it is too late: he has begun and it would take a dozen horses to drag him off the job. All you can do at this point is retire gracefully to your office in the faint hope that he does know something about what he is doing or that by some miracle he will find and fix the fault.

On your return, your heart will sink as you see Harry surrounded by more bits of machinery than you have ever seen in one place. In great trepidation you ask 'Well?'

'Just as I thought,' Harry will say, 'your triple phase circuit diode distributor board is shot to hell.'

'Really? Is that good or bad?'

What can he do about it? Has he got another one in his pocket? When you ask him what the next move is, he says with complete confidence, 'Oh, it's not a big job, now that I've stripped it down for the engineer.' So saying, he picks up his tools, replaces them in the correct pockets and leaves with a reassuring, 'They can be quite tricky, these babies ... if you don't know what you're doing. Fortunately I didn't come across any major snags.'

Good old Harry. You can always rely on him to get you out of a jam. When the engineer does arrive he throws a fit over the state of the machine. He then spends six hours at an extortionate charge rate rebuilding what Harry has ripped apart, only to discover that the fault is a bad connection of the lead with the plug. When you are coherent enough to speak to Harry and tell him that there was nothing wrong with the triple phase circuit diode distributor board, he will simply smile knowingly and say, 'Well, it may be okay at the moment, but it's only a matter of time. I've never seen one so bad.'

THE PROFESSIONAL

Professional experts come in all shapes and sizes, some of them claiming expertise in areas so specialised that you might suspect them of being able to write the sum of their knowledge on the back of a postage stamp. Of course, by claiming to be expert in such arcana, they know that there is no-one in a position to challenge them. Whenever you come across such a person show him the door immediately because he is almost certainly some species of conman. And whatever you do, make sure he does not find his way to your boss's office, where he will be given a warm welcome and a ready ear.

In the larger organisations or conglomerates, one of the worst types of expert that you will encounter is the one from corporate headquarters, because:

- he is privy to much more information and at a higher level in the organisation than you are

- he has authority from the top (to which even your boss feels it expedient to defer)
- he has talked to your boss first and been given the low-down on you and your department

Regardless of the reasons for his presence in your organisation, the head office expert will certainly regard it as his duty to have a snoop around and report back to base. This is a very dangerous situation for a survivor as these experts are usually noted for their eccentricity and snap judgements; you will not have had a chance to work on him as you have done on your boss and he may well misinterpret what he sees and hears in your department.

It goes without saying that whatever you are doing within his field of expertise, you will be doing it the wrong way. The expert must find something wrong everywhere he goes, otherwise he cannot continue claiming to be an expert. He reasons thus: 'If managers continually get things right, they must know almost as much as I do, therefore they too are experts, meaning everybody is an expert. But if everybody is an expert, nobody is an expert. Including me.' It is important to realize that, along with ego, one of the prime motivators for the expert, as well as in management, is self-justification, commonly known as 'covering your backside' or 'laying six feet of concrete'. Witness the scurry of managers to clear out files, check memos or rewrite history when the boss casually mentions some long-forgotten but poorly executed project.

In order to come out on top in your dealings with the expert from corporate headquarters, you must have a range of tactics at your disposal and use whichever one is most appropriate to the situation:

- take pains to ensure that he has no reason to visit you. For instance, always complete and return his pointless forms on time, even if you have to invent the data; he probably won't notice anyway, but if he does he'll blame it on his computer which generally produces garbage. As many managers may suspect, most of the weekly or monthly returns they are required to complete are thrown in the bin unread on reaching corporate headquarters. The data is only required as a justification for their existence. Apart from that, what the hell would they do over there all day?

- when a visit from a head office expert is unavoidable, try and find out its purpose in advance. Then you can prepare for him by getting ready the information he will require and sending him on his way quickly. You should also give people in slack sections of your department the day off; dust off your pile of computer print-outs and strew them all over your desk; have one of your staff interrupt every ten minutes with a major problem which you will consider for a moment then solve with a flash of inspiration; arrange a meeting with your people to start before the expert is due to arrive then claim that you did not know he was coming. All of your carefully prepared scenarios will appear all the more efficient for being spontaneous
- *in extremis*, and on a pre-arranged signal, you can have a colleague 'crash' the computer system or produce obvious garbage, then you say to the expert, 'When they installed this thing, I said to your guys over there, "Shouldn't I keep some manual records as well? What happens if the thing goes down?" But as usual, they knew best.'

Generally speaking, you only have to get the better of a head office expert once for him to avoid you for ever more, or at least deal with you at arm's length. However, you must be careful to give the impression that it was inadvertent; if he thinks that you did it deliberately he could put the wrong word in the right ear at a high level and you could be heading for the front door for the last time. In the main, if you treat him like a little tin god, ask his advice and give him the respect he thinks he deserves, you should be able to avoid any major disasters.

Of the experts who come from outside your organisation, undoubtedly the two most obnoxious are the computer expert and the management consultant, the latter being the only known example of a professional who claims to be expert in everything.

The computer expert is a particularly virulent form of corporate virus for which there is no known cure. The major threat which he poses is that of boredom if he talks to you for any more than ninety seconds – this should give you enough time to say, 'Thank you very much. No, I don't understand one word of what you are saying, but I'm sure I don't need it.'

Do not attempt to appear knowledgeable by saying things like, 'And how would that interface with our present systems?' as this will only encourage him. You will encounter many experts in management, of whom the computer whizz-kid is the undoubted master of egospeak, having more neologisms and esoteric terminology at his command than five other experts put together. The most vociferous exponent of this is the computer salesman. Computer salesmen are only exceeded in unctuousness by morticians and bed salesmen and it is surely more than a coincidence that in each of their hands you end up prostrate.

The computer expert speaks a peculiar dialect of egospeak known as Desperanto. This is terminal in most cases and extremely contagious to the unwary (an early sign of infection is the use of the letter 'k' in place of the word 'thousands' when referring to monetary amounts). While terms such as 'hardware' and 'software' are fairly straightforward, 'firmware' may prove a little more difficult. When it comes to bits, bytes (of the kilo, mega, and giga variety), databases, formatted disks, RS232 ports and local area networks, your knowledge and your patience are running out fast. Throw in a few red herrings, not to say misnomers, such as 'user-friendly' and 'intelligent terminal' and you will be ready for verbal if not physical violence. And that's only the hardware; he hasn't started on his software spiel yet, with its 'interfaces', 'menu-drive' and 'Unix-operated'.

There is absolutely no point in attempting to beat the computer expert on his own terms; you will certainly fail, as he can talk louder and longer and can invent new terminology faster than you can. You must attack him in his areas of weakness. The following methods should prove useful.

- demand that he demonstrate what his hardware and software can do, using examples from your department rather than data he provides. He may leave to consult his colleagues on the exact format and the chances are that you will never see him again. Nine times out of ten the computer salesman will assure you that his system will do whatever you require of it; and by the time you find out differently, i.e. after you have paid for it, you will discover that he has moved to another computer company

(computer salesmen change their jobs more often than Italians change their government)

- ask him to sign a declaration that the programs his company is currently writing will be ready to be used by you on the promised date. If he has told you 'December', ask him 'December of which year?'
- despite their protestations to the contrary, computer experts know very little about management (it is said that they know very little about anything else). Question your expert closely, demanding that he answer in plain English. After a long silence he will leave, saying that he must return to base for re-programming
- tell him that your budget for the computer project is extremely low and that your company would not entertain a leasing agreement. You won't see him for dust!
- send Harry to speak to him. About a month later you will hear that the computer expert has lost his missionary zeal, given up his job and taken a post as a toilet attendant in a quiet part of town

While the computer expert can be annoying and troublesome at times, the management consultant is a more terrifying beast altogether. Sanctioned by the chief executive, he has the freedom to go where he pleases, poking and prying into anything that takes his fancy. He is a man with a bag of solutions in search of a problem and if he hasn't got a solution then you can't have a problem. But let him discover an area of management for which he has a few patent remedies and he will find problems that you never knew you had. Never mind that you don't think they are problems; he will soon demonstrate why they are, how he will fix them and what a reasonable fee he will charge for doing so. Moreover, once he has got his feet under the table he will be very difficult to shift because he will then have ample time to turn up yet more 'problems'. He may end up being with the organisation so long that a newcomer might be justified in asking, 'That guy in the pinstripe suit and silk tie, does he work here?' – to which you should reply 'Oh no, he's a management consultant.' More often than not there will be a team of them (known as 'a charge of consultants'), wandering all over the

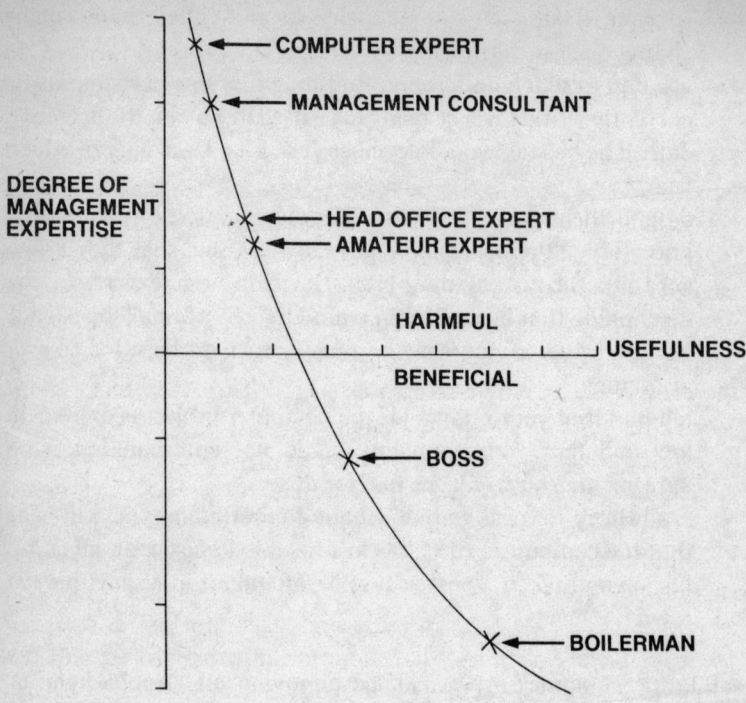

department and making life hell for the unfortunate manager, who cannot keep an eye on all of them simultaneously.

Like any other experts, the best way to deal with consultants is to try and ensure that they are not engaged in the first place, but do not be lulled into a false sense of security by thinking that if you have no obvious problems in your department your boss won't call them in. The moment you find out that your boss has been talking to consultants you must get to work on him by:

– pointing out the loss of face he will suffer by admitting that he is unable to run the organisation himself
– showing him that the fee rate he has been quoted is per day and not per week as he thought
– telling him that, if questioned by a consultant you will feel

obliged to tell the man absolutely everything which has happened recently, and reminding your boss that a copy of the report will certainly be seen by the main board of directors

Despite these arguments, your boss may not be convinced. After all, why should he listen to you now when he has never done so before? He is the man who will greet as messianic and rush to implement those solutions put forward by the consultant which you have been advocating for years without success. So, when you come whistling into your office one morning to find a management consultant sitting at your desk going through your papers, what can you do? Basically, there are only two approaches to adopt: you can either refuse to co-operate, or you can co-operate him to death.

In using the first approach of course, you must not be seen to be uncooperative, as the consultant will merely go whining to your boss. You must agree to talk to him and provide the required facts and figures, then ensure that you have enough operational crises to prevent you complying with his requests, accompanied by profuse apologies and assurances that you are eager to assist in any way you can. He has only a limited time to finish his project and will probably report to your boss that everything is rosy in your department, rather than admit that he failed to get the salient facts.

Overwhelming him with co-operation will certainly throw him off balance as he will not be used to this. You must spend every possible moment with him, producing figures by the ream, snowing him under with documentation and asking for his advice on every conceivable management topic. He will be unable to resist this and will happily spend precious hours recounting his experiences and expounding the latest management theories – for consultants are the carriers of the 'fad' bacteria developed in the laboratories of the management theorists. If you are in manufacturing, prepare to hear about materials requirements planning and just-in-time manufacture; if in administration, it will be management by walking around or one minute managing. (Unfortunately, this takes a little longer than one minute to explain.)

The single most effective way of 'nobbling' a pushy consultant is to tell him everything about all the systems and practices in your department, leaving out one significant section. Then, on his last day in the organisation and preferably as you are shaking hands and saying goodbye, casually mention the part which you have left out and say that it is just as well that he did not want to know about that, as it would take at least a week to cover it thoroughly. If you do adopt this approach, make sure that you have a chair and a glass of water on hand!

As in other areas of management, the fully qualified fox should have little trouble dealing with experts, because he is prepared to utilise the underhand methods which ordinary (non-surviving) managers eschew. Handling experts brings out the very essence of foxery; having successfully resisted them, in the nicest possible way, both the experts and your boss will still be saying what a great guy you are.

9 BOSS MANAGEMENT

'The trouble with the US Army is, there are too many chiefs and not enough Indians.'

General George Custer

Of all the skills that need to be learned and practised by the would-be survivor in the corporate jungle, such as the managing of resources and the handling of staff, the most vital is the ability to manage your boss, because ultimately it is against him that you must survive; he is the gamekeeper to your poacher. There are many types of manager, so we must attempt to pick out their key characteristics, classify them and formulate methods of dealing with each type.

Since the earliest days of management investigators and theorists, there has been a steady stream of literature on the subject of leadership. Many of the theories put forward have been put into practice in organisations with varying degrees of success, but now all of this has been made redundant by the recent findings of Professor Milo Trashe. His recent brilliant paper *Boss Behaviour in a Hostile Ambience* (ed. J. J. Skivington) puts forward his findings and his thesis of the underlying psychology.

From the study data three basic types of boss emerged: the opportunist, the missionary and the hermit. While all bosses have certain characteristics in common, their attributes and actions, and therefore the defences required against each of the three types, are quite different. From the various characteristics outlined by Professor Trashe you should attempt to classify your boss so that you can then formulate a strategy and take the most effective action for your own survival.

THE OPPORTUNIST

As his name suggests, the opportunist never misses a trick. His primary motivation in life is to get to the top and he is not too concerned about how he achieves it. Not for him the long wait for dead men's shoes (unless he is instrumental in emptying them!); he is a man in a hurry, and the only reason a management fox should get close to him is to throw a banana skin in his path.

The opportunist probably obtained his position as boss under somewhat false pretences, having expanded and exaggerated his qualifications and experience. Indeed it may well be that his qualifications are almost non-existent and his experience limited, but being adept at job interviews he would be quite capable of persuading the interviewers that his fifteen years' experience in ten different industries was just what they needed (like all good salesmen he sells the sizzle and not the steak). He would say all the right things and appear to know all the right people. Always being in a hurry to get to the next stage, he never takes much time at any one thing, including college, university or business school. He is a doer rather than a thinker (he says), although he is likely to consider himself the greatest strategist and tactician since Napoleon, but he has no particular philosophy of life or management except that a moving target is the hardest to hit.

The major weapon in the opportunist's armoury is appearance and because of this he will certainly want to embrace some kind of corporate culture, though he will not be fussy which one. If there's a fad going ... he's your man! Management by Objectives, Matrix Management or Nude Management, if it looks good, it does you good. Thanks very much, he'll have it ... at least until the next fad comes along. At heart he is an impressionist, with a quick dab here and another dab there, stand back and it all looks fine. But come up too close and you can certainly see the joins.

Being concerned primarily with appearance, your opportunist boss will be a snappy dresser and will often keep a spare suit, shirts and ties in his office so that he can change in the evening before going directly to some social function. He's all go, with his corporate and social life inextricably mixed. His office (or more likely 'executive suite') will be furnished and decorated with the best that the organisation's money can buy (having it redecorated and furnished was probably his first action after being appointed), with a mahogany desk, leather swivel chair, built-in personal computer which he doesn't know how to use, cocktail cabinet which he does, and a carpet with a pile so deep that it tickles your ankles each time you walk across it. *En suite*, there will be a toilet and shower room, replete with six different types of eau-de-Cologne (only losers wear aftershave). He will have a phone in his car and another one in his briefcase, as he likes nothing better than to cut a dash by using it in public places to cancel two pints of milk with his milkman, under the guise of cancelling an order on a foreign supplier.

This is a man who likes to see and be seen around his empire (his word), and indeed he can often be observed striding along corridors, popping into offices, breezing through the production area, all the while smiling and nodding to all and sundry as if he actually knew them all personally. If someone asks him a question or outlines a problem the opportunist boss will nod sagely, and then reply, 'Well, I was thinking that very thing the other day. I haven't quite got all my thoughts together on this yet, but if you can leave it with me for a couple of days, I'll get back to you and we'll thrash this one out.' And before his questioner can reply, 'But you've said that three times in the last four weeks,' the opportunist is off with a cheery wave. Now and then he will sweep into your office and ask you one or two pointed questions about your department, such as, 'How many of your people are in today?' Watch his eyes as you answer: they will take on a glazed look as he thinks up a question for the next manager.

When called upon, the opportunist is very swift and sure about making decisions. Simply tell him the problem and he gives you a decision; no doubts, no debate, no alternatives. Marvellous. But when it proves to be wrong, you try getting him to admit that he gave it. Making decisions about the workforce is a speciality of the opportunist and given half a chance he will distribute your labour for you: he will have the carpenter and the painter round at his house fitting a new kitchen and redecorating the lounge, while the handyman is digging over his garden and the maintenance engineer is tuning the engine in his speedboat. One thing's for sure: there's no idle time around the opportunist's organisation. His love of appearances, however, will not extend to his timekeeping, as his starting and finishing times are often erratic. On some occasions he will be in the office well before anyone else and on others he won't arrive until near lunchtime, with no explanation being sought or given. Usually he will take a one and a half or two hour 'working' lunch in the best restaurant in town (he is the boss, after all).

Of the three types of boss the opportunist is probably the easiest for you to deal with, as his emphasis on appearance can work to your advantage, and besides, he is the nearest thing there is to a fox without actually being one! As long as you give the appearance of success, he won't be too concerned how you go about it. The biggest problem you will have with this type of boss is that he will constantly have you wasting your valuable management time on crack-brained schemes which he will abandon in favour of something new as soon as you have brought them to fruition. In order to counter this management mania, Milo Trashe suggests a number of courses of action.

- Wait until the opportunist leaves the organisation, as the natural life cycle of his jobs is usually around two years. He can rarely resist the opportunity of a bigger and better position, and while this could be provided from within the organisation, another factor comes into play which precludes this. The opportunist boss is not a good manager but he has long since learned that in any senior management post it takes at least two years to be found out, by which time he has had a settling-in period, an organising period, an experimental period, a consolidation period and a reappraisal period. By the time disquiet is being shown about his lack of performance, the opportunist will have moved on to greater things: if he does not linger on each stepping stone the corporate sharks cannot bite his ankles. So, if you can play the waiting game you will soon be rid of him, although he is likely to leave a trail of devastation in his wake.
- You can of course play him at his own game, i.e. spot the truth. As he is very big on appearances, give him some. Slap a few posters up around the place, such as 'Time is money, so get your ass in gear', 'Before leaving the premises please empty your pockets of all company products as we may need them to sell to

customers', or 'Silence is golden, so shut up and cash in'. Flood him with memos on every conceivable subject which say very little and commit you to less. The opportunist usually mistakes movement for action, so anything that moves, start a committee for it, and for anything that doesn't move, appoint a sub-committee, with copies of all minutes to the boss.

- The opportunist loves experts and listens to them avidly, picking up bits of information with which to impress other people. You know plenty of experts, in fact you are trying to get rid of some, so send Harry round to see him. That should get both of them out of your hair for a while. When an expert comes from Head Office or from outside the organisation, plead ignorance and tell him that your boss is the man he's after.

- He believes in behaviour modification but is as subtle in its application as a rampaging elephant; because he thinks that everyone is motivated in the same way as he is, to encourage competition among his managers, he offers exciting incentives such as a weekend break for two at a casino, tickets to a wrestling match or a framed portrait of himself in directorial pose. As he is such a great advocate of competition, provide him with some by telling him that one of his rivals in the organisation is turning in a great performance, is getting on with the Chairman like a house on fire, has made derogatory remarks about your esteemed boss, and vice versa. Then they can really have a go at each other while you sit innocently on the sidelines holding the jackets.

- An annual appraisal will always be carried out for each manager by the opportunist. It may be too good to miss, but all he's really interested in is picking out one or two adverse trends in your performance and using them against you. He will gloss over everything else. You must therefore have all your 'facts' at your fingertips. Bore him with long-winded and irrelevant explanations of incidents over the preceding year, so that the allocated time for the appraisal is used up; contest everything he says and have a plausible alternative; set the pace at the beginning by explaining why the 'failures' were in fact thinly disguised successes; and as he admires opportunism so much, get in early with a substantial salary demand, thereby requiring him to justify his refusal (if he has just returned from one of those two-hour lunches, he might just agree to it).

THE MISSIONARY

What fuels the missionary is his desire to be the best manager that ever was, running the best organisation, using every management method and technique known to man. He concerns himself with everything under his command and is truly a man with a mission: if you are not a believer he will spare no effort to convert you. The academic aspects of management fascinate him and this will be reflected in his qualifications. He will certainly have at least one degree and an MBA (but if it's not from Harvard he won't mention it) and will be a member of every possible professional institute, with a great row of letters after his name, making his business cards so long that he has to carry them under his arm. The only way that a missionary will obtain a boss's position will be by sheer merit (yes, there are such people around). He is Mr Smart. He will overwhelm the interviewers with his knowledge and earnestness, exhorting them to embrace his management philosophy and outline the transformation it would make in their organisation. Dazzled by his missionary zeal they will rush to sign him up, then regret it at leisure.

When it comes to corporate culture, the missionary could have invented it. He has read every management book under the sun (including execrable translations from Japanese management books explaining how it is all done with raw fish and work ethics), and uses all the junk phrases like 'people are your greatest asset', and 'having the will to win'. He will set up 'task forces' and practise 'management by walking around'. Rather than tell you that he wants you to achieve certain corporate objectives, he will say that what is needed between you and the organisation is 'goal congruence' and not the 'goal dissonance' that has recently been manifested (and no, he's not pulling your leg – he really means it!).

The missionary will tell you that what must be practised is 'intrapreneuring' ('Looking for diamonds in the corporate navel and finding fluff', says Professor Trashe). But why can't he just tell you, 'What we need is to kick a few asses around here'?

The main problem posed by the missionary is that he is so unfailingly earnest about everything. He actually believes all that stuff (as opposed to the opportunist, who merely affects to believe it for the sake of appearances), and thinks that he can put it into practice, for, like all idealists, he is naïve about human nature. As part of his corporate culture the missionary will certainly be very concerned about dress, both his own and that of his staff, requiring that everyone wears some kind of uniform, either overalls for the workforce or dark suits, white shirts and striped ties for his managers. When the air-conditioning breaks down in a heat wave he will sit in his office as if it was an Arctic ice-floe, not a bead of sweat on him, while a lesser mortal (i.e. you), will drag himself around like a wet rag, scared to ask if he can open his collar. 'Hot?' he will say, 'Hot? What has that got to do with anything? I'm trying to run a business here and you want to run around like a tramp.'

With the amount of memos this boss creates he is the lumber industry's best customer. Memos, plans, summaries and agendas fly from his pen like pages from a hack writer, to cover notice boards and desks and bring cries of 'We give in!' from his beleaguered managers; the pen is indeed mightier than the kick in the ass.

The missionary's office will be tastefully decorated but functional, with a large area being given over to his management books, one of which he will press upon you each time you enter the hallowed chamber. However, he will spend little time in his office as he is an advocate of the 'see and be seen' method, i.e. 'management by walking around'. In offices and on the shopfloor he will engage in earnest conversation with everyone he meets, remembering each person's name and what was said the last time they spoke (nobody else will). You won't be able to turn around before he is at your elbow, enquiring, advising, encouraging; in the 'pain-in-the-neck' category he gets ten out of ten.

In the missionary's opinion, decision-making is no time for snap judgements or intuition (i.e. he cannot make decisions). Every aspect of the problem must be isolated, examined, compared and evaluated, with every possibility taken into consideration. This makes it almost impossible to get a decision out of the man while the issue is still current, as he will go into retreat over the smallest thing. In the meantime you will have taken the decision yourself and actioned it without telling him, in order to pull your department's nuts out of the fire. This is what the missionary would call a 'damage limitation exercise'.

As with all bosses, the type and duration of the lunch which the missionary takes is indicative of his management style, (what Trashe called the 'Repast Factor'). Generally he will take lunch in the organisation's cafeteria, always opting for the balanced diet and no doubt having calculated the calorific value of each dish to two decimal places. As like as not, he will jog from his office to lunch and back again, always using the stairs in preference to the lift. Every day, in every way, he must set an example, therefore he starts his lunch after everyone else and finishes before them. You won't catch him going for a two-hour lunch and swaying back to the office as if he'd just spent two days at a beer festival. When he brings his lunch over to your table you can forget about eating yours; after he has poured out his morning's deliberations, you just won't feel like it. And if he ever takes you out to lunch then beware, because it probably means that you have not managed to survive after all.

To handle the missionary boss successfully, evasive action will be to no avail as he will hound you to the ends of the organisation, trap you in a corner and preach you his gospel until you sink to the floor a quivering wreck. What you must do is take the opposite tack and come out fighting. Seek his advice at every possible opportunity and on every subject, regardless of how minor it is; camp in his office and demand an explanation of the philosophy behind each book (naturally you will never read what he gives you, simply make the pages look dog-earned and put a few random pencil notes in the margins, such as: 'Yes, but somewhat naïve in the context of this subject'. That should fox him!); 'phone him constantly; send him telexes asking advice whenever he is away on business; and swamp him with memos.

You will find that one of the missionary's hobby-horses is good communications and so you must tell him everything that you think he would like to hear as opposed to what actually happened in the greatest possible detail. Overwhelm him with information and communication and within a short time he will indicate that he could possibly live without quite so much of it. This is your chance, as you can then steadily reduce all communication with him until he is only aware of your existence by the submission of your monthly expenses. The key to dealing effectively with the missionary boss is given in Professor Trashe's paper *Boss Behaviour in a Hostile Ambience*, where he states that, 'Once the missionary believes that he has made a management convert he will move on to the next management heathen, leaving the new disciple to spread the word among his people. This is his primary motivation.' So the answer is clear: you must give all the expected responses and convince him that you have joined his flock. Tell him that you are a fast learner and that you not only understand but embrace his philosophy. With any luck he will turn his attention to one of your managerial colleagues; an arch-rival will be seriously compromised, you will be free of harassment and will be able to revert to your former ways.

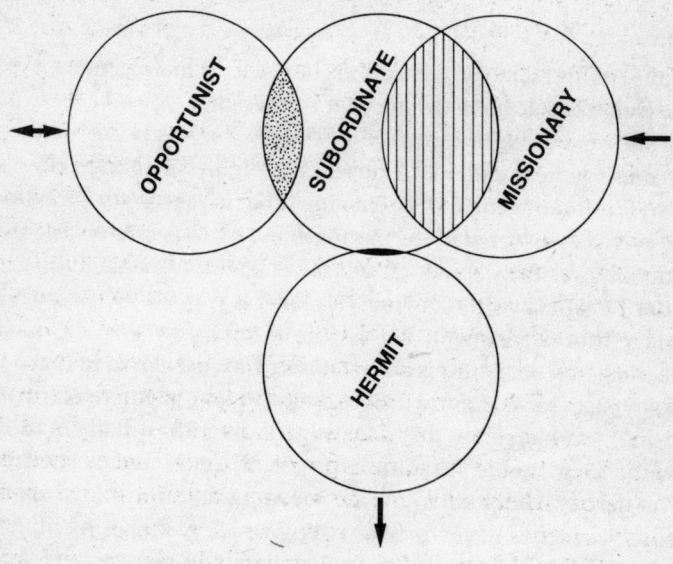

THE HERMIT

Here is the boss you have been looking for, the perfect complement to the management fox. Described by Milo Trashe as 'a misanthrope, much given to secrecy', all he really wants is a quiet life. The fact is that he never wanted to be in management at all and would much rather be a lighthouse keeper or in some similar occupation where he would be out of touch with his fellow man. 'It quickly became apparent during our observations,' Trashe tells us, 'that the hermit would be difficult to assess, as except for fleeting glimpses he was rarely seen in action.'

It is more than likely that the hermit will have no academic qualifications whatsoever, either in management or in anything else. This type of boss normally obtains his position in one of three ways:

- he is a relative or close family friend of one of the directors
- the Chairman recognised a kindred spirit (i.e. a fellow incompetent), and wishing to retain consistency in his management team, appointed the hermit
- he was mistakenly given the position after the application forms for it were mixed up with those for a junior supervisor's job for which he did apply

Because of his lack of qualifications or top level management experience (some people have twenty years' experience – he is likely to have had one year's experience twenty times!), he has never developed any management skills and survives solely by his native cunning. His style is 'management by exception', that is, it is pretty exceptional if he ever gets involved in the management of his people or resources. If you are ever foolish enough to ask his advice on some managerial matter he will say, 'I'm paying you [as if it was his own money] to manage that department, not to run to me every time you have a little problem.' So, your biggest customer has just closed his account, two suppliers have stopped deliveries due to non-payment of invoices and your workforce has just downed tools over the quality of the tea from the tea machine? That's not a problem, that's an opportunity . . .

The hermit would not know the meaning of the words 'corporate culture', as he has never done anything which would bring him into contact with it. Management books are anathema to him, as he has neither the determination nor the inclination to read one through to the end. In fact, he has read very few books in his life and if anyone was ever to suggest that he was bought a book as a birthday present the answer would probably be, 'No, I think he's got one of those already.' Because of his own failings in this department the thing that annoys him more than anything else in management is an academic and he will not entertain one in any shape or form. He would not know a management game from a poker game and thinks that management schools are simply breeding grounds for management guerillas who are sent out to terrorise the world of industry and commerce. Don't ever look to the hermit for a lead in style or philosophy because it certainly will not be forthcoming.

The hermit is in no way interested in appearances, which is why he never makes any! His dress is likely to be sloppy, unconventional, even outlandish; he may wear a large wollen pullover under his suit jacket, a sports coat with elbow patches, brown shoes with a navy suit and vice versa, and clothes which generally look as if they had been rejected by Oxfam. As for his office, it is a shambles and his filing system is the despair of his secretary – instead of filing cabinets he has piles of letters, memos, computer print-outs and unread magazines stacked on the floor (he works on the principle that if the sender is not pressing for a reply to a letter or memo within three months he simply dumps them unread). Not one square inch of the top of his desk can be seen as it is obliterated by memos, letters, reports and unpaid invoices from suppliers, and he will blame the mess on his secretary who, he says, is incompetent in filing.

Naturally the hermit is rarely if ever seen out of his office except when the fire bell rings, because in this way he avoids getting involved in the day-by-day management of his organisation. If he ever does venture into offices or onto the shop-floor (probably because he has taken a wrong turning and got lost), one of his staff is likely to enquire of him, 'Can I help you, Mr ... ?' By the same token, except for those managers who report directly to him, the hermit will not know the names of any of his staff and will generally refer to individuals as '... our friend here ...', '... this man ...' or '... this woman ...'. People are certainly not his greatest asset but a continual source of annoyance to him, and he regards them in much the same way as he does customers.

There are two principal ways that this type of executive keeps in touch with events in his organisation. One is his extensive use of the grapevine, with information being conveyed to him by his secretary. If you could persuade her to feed him spurious information (i.e. more spurious than that which he gets already), you could place yourself in a commanding position. Not only does he receive news of all the dirt on everyone in the organisation, but he believes it and acts accordingly. His second method of keeping tabs is to read all incoming and outgoing mail; every scrap of paper is scanned by him, and although he may make no immediate comment he will mentally file away the information for possible future use. In the case of outgoing mail, if he takes exception to a letter someone has written he will simply throw it in the bin, leaving the unfortunate manager expecting a reply to a letter which was never sent! His actions tend to be illogical and arbitrary and a major problem in dealing with him is his unpredictability.

The hermit boss is automatically against anything you might care to propose, especially if it involves spending any money, so you will have to take pains to persuade him into agreement, even with those things that appear to you to be vitally and self-evidently important. His primary attribute is inertia, and this applies in particular to his decision-making. Not infrequently he will ask you, 'What do you think?' Then, when you have given the matter due consideration and told him your opinion, he will do the opposite of what you have recommended. And when you make considered suggestions to him, regarding the acquisition of a piece of capital equipment, for instance, he will wave you away and say that it is far too expensive.... but let someone from outside the organisation tell him of this marvellous piece of technology and he will immediately sign on the dotted line, despite the fact that it is now three times as expensive as when you first suggested it a year before. The fact that it is not in your budget is irrelevant; he will simply order it and pay for it, then chop something of equivalent value from your budget (you can be sure it won't come out of his!). If you later protest to him, he will say, 'If I remember correctly, it was you that suggested this in the first place. Now that I've put my neck on the line by sanctioning a capital requisition which is not in the budget, you're backing off. I think you and I should have a serious talk about your job attitude.'

It is difficult to classify the hermit using Trashe's 'Repast Factor' as nobody can say for sure where he goes for lunch or indeed if he takes any lunch at all. He simply disappears from the office at all times of the day without telling anyone where he is going and when he will return. According to Milo Trashe, 'The hermit is a true non-manager. Much more research will have to be undertaken in order to discover the underlying causes of this type of behaviour, given the complex series of competing emotions involved in this type of character.'

As indicated earlier, the hermit is the best type of boss that a management fox can have, but of course he is not without his drawbacks. For instance, you cannot question his basic strategy or tactics at your annual performance appraisal, because he never has either. Neither can you attempt to construct a departmental budget with a built-in leeway for various contingencies; your boss will draw it up and may not even tell you how it is made up. All you will hear is, 'You can't have that. It's not in the budget.' Again, communications are pointless, as he ignores official lines and prefers to rely on his grapevine. However, you can make use of this to plant information you wish him to hear and, as he thinks he is getting it without your knowledge, he will believe it implicitly.

Being a pessimist by nature, the hermit does not believe in any kind of behaviour modification, saying that 'leopards do not change their spots'. You are therefore unlikely to be bothered by any kind of management development or training schemes, as your boss will rightly regard them as a waste of time and money. There is only one way to do things: the hermit's way. Professor Trashe states, 'While the hermit appears to delegate completely to his subordinates, in fact he merely has his people on a very long lead, controlling them both financially and by dominance of the communications system. Although he practises management by stealth and appears to be incompetent, he is often quite effective in the running of his organisation.' Clearly, the hermit can often be perverse and unpredictable and can take a major decision on a mere whim, but having taken it, he will defend it to the very last, come hell, high water or corporate disaster. The most effective way to counteract his negative tendencies is to keep your information system working efficiently, so that you do at least get some information beforehand of which way he is going to move.

The drawbacks of living with this kind of boss are generally far outweighed by the benefits, and as long as he stays in his hermitage your chances of managing to survive should be very high.

10 FIGURING IT OUT

'If it's a violin you want, go see an orchestra; you want a fiddle, I know a tame accountant.'

Sam Goldwyn

You need only look at the financial press or the contents of the average manager's In tray to see that, in whatever sector of the economy an organisation is operating, everything it does is eventually reduced to figures. This presents an obvious difficulty for a management fox because he will be subjected to an impression of precision which is alien to his nature. The fox thrives on vagueness, and figures in black and white are too precise by half (in most organisations the amount of figures that are precise probably is about half).

While you will obviously have to have *some* ability with figures (even if it is only to know which ones to invent), you must bear in mind that in management, as in life, all figures are relative and not nearly as important as your boss and the accountants in your organisation would have you believe. The ultimate aim of figures in any commercial enterprise is merely to determine the organisation's profit or loss. The notion here is that profit is generally regarded as being good and loss as being bad, unless, that is, the board of directors, the accountants or the tax consultants decide that it should temporarily be otherwise. Any organisation which manages to break even would naturally be regarded with grave suspicion.

It generally helps to keep the shareholders happy (i.e. off the backs of the directors at the annual general meeting) if the enterprise makes a modest profit about once every three or four years. Anything more substantial or regular than this and they may begin to expect it every year, placing an intolerable extra burden on the hard-pressed management. However, it is not necessary to realise any profit, provided it can be shown that even if the organisation's assets are not actually increasing, they are at least not being eroded by inflation (meaning currency inflation, not the inflated figures of creative accountants) or the depredations of spendthrift managers.

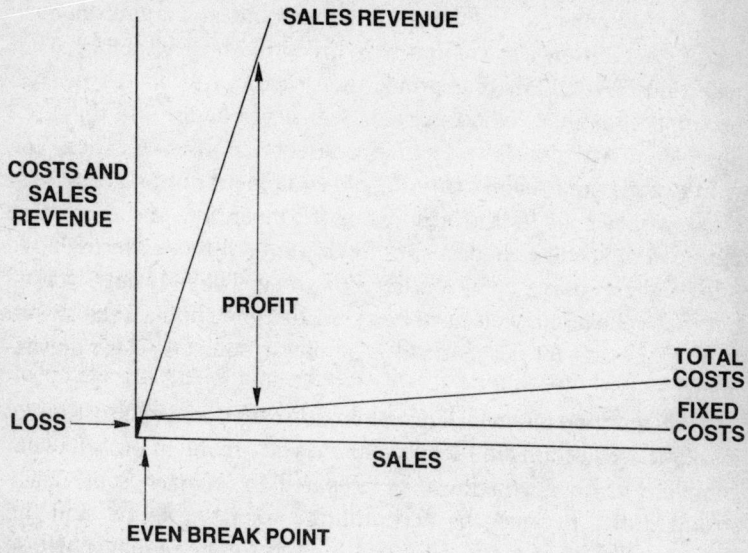

In the majority of cases shareholders and governments fail to realise the basic economic facts of life; that once they have put money into an enterprise ('investment' is a misnomer, as this implies that some return is expected), the directors regard it as fair game for all sorts of dubious purposes. Directors have often been accused of treating corporate money as if it was their own. Not a bit of it. If it was their own money they would certainly be much more careful with it!

Examples of this type of *laissez-faire* situation (which is in fact the management fox's natural habitat) can be seen in many organisations, with directors awarding themselves handsome pay rises and large new cars when neither of these things are justified by corporate performance. 'What has that got to do with anything?' the chairman cries, 'We have to offer the best remuneration to get the right people on the board.' Comments like 'He should be on the board: nailed to it,' are not relevant here. The question is, who are the right people? Well, they are probably his friends, relatives, old school pals or anyone a slick head hunter has talked him into taking on for a fat fee. And after all, these people could up and leave for another sinecure at the drop of a hat, and then where would we be?

Observe your board of directors when politicians and economists next urge industry and commerce to invest in new technology. They will send up a chorus of approval then rush out to buy themselves personal computers whose screens will never be lit, and the latest limousines with 24-valve engines and computerised electrics. You won't catch these fellows running old equipment until it drops: they know what's good for the business. In the meantime, just try getting approval to spend a modest sum having a vital typewriter repaired (although, of course, being a trainee fox you will already have worked out that you should wait until everyone has gone home, then switch your typewriter for an identical good one in someone else's department).

If you mention financial figures in one breath then you must surely mention accountants in the next (and if you are intent on achieving complete foxhood you must be prepared to stomach some fairly strong stuff!), because the accountant makes the figures and the figures make the accountant. For the unfortunate manager whose only wish is to survive, the terminology and techniques of financial accounting present something of a hurdle, but you can expect no help from the accountants as they almost rival the computer experts in the art of egospeak. Wander into any accountant's office to ask for assistance with some minor financial matter and before you know where you are he will be hitting you with phrases like 'total absorption costing', 'break-even analysis' and 'marginal costing', with an opinion as to their merits in any given situation. Even if you tell him that it all appears to be pretty damned marginal to you and would he please cut the crap and explain to you why your department has to bear such a large proportion of head office overheads, you will be too late; he is already off, his alpha-numeric egospeak pouring from his lips as he lectures you on capital investment appraisal and in which circumstances one should use the payback or the discounted cash flow methods. Then, when he has you thoroughly confused, he will feint with a 'sensitivity analysis' and finish you off with a quick 'cumulative probabilities'.

The accountants would have you believe that investment

appraisal techniques are the modern equivalent of alchemists' recipes, but in reality they are generally no more than a means of justifying an impulse buy by the chairman or one of the directors. One of these techniques will certainly be used to decide whether or not you can spend £1,000 on a much-needed piece of equipment, but will not be used to evaluate the site of a new factory and head-quarters which is chosen by the chairman and his wife because she is not prepared to move house yet again. 'Yes, yes,' he will say soothingly, 'figures are all very well in their place, but sometimes a qualitative judgement is called for, and I just have a feeling about this site.'

Because figures are used in management accounting you must not make the mistake of thinking that this makes it an exact science; in the hands of a skilled operator the figures can be made to say whatever is required. All the more reason for you as a survivor to know something of the basics of this black art. (By the way, you should at all times attempt to deal solely in percentages, as this gives the useful impression that nobody is working with real money; after all, you cannot recklessly spend a percentage.) The two principal devices used to record and monitor the progress of an organisation are the Balance Sheet and the Profit and Loss Account.

THE BALANCE SHEET

The Balance Sheet shows the supposed financial position of the enterprise at a particular point in time by listing its Assets and Liabilities. Items such as machines, furniture and vehicles are termed Fixed Assets (though naturally not so fixed that they cannot be purloined by management for personal use), and are generally valued at historical, some would say hysterical, cost. Current Assets such as Debtors, and Cash and Stock, which present a whole range of possibilities to the creative accountant, are also listed. From these are subtracted Current Liabilities (apart from the Board of Directors, that is, who have no known worth), Taxation, Creditors and Pro-posed Dividends – which is usually good for a laugh in the boardroom. Net Assets are then set against Capital, Reserves and Long-term Liabilities (depending on the length of his service contract, this may include the Chairman).

The Balance Sheet is often regarded as being a snapshot of the business and for this many managements are grateful, as it is a set-piece and shows no action, but paradoxically it reflects the true situation of some enterprises quite well. The Profit and Loss Account, on the other hand, is more like a film or play, carefully stage-managed and rehearsed for presentation to the unsuspecting audience.

THE PROFIT AND LOSS ACCOUNT

In many businesses today the Profit and Loss Account is given undue significance. This is for historical reasons, since before the age of enlightened management untempered capitalism insisted that some kind of profit was made every single year. With the advent of more sophisticated management techniques and philosophies, stemming from recent discoveries in social and organisational psychology (i.e. that people are not overly keen on hard work), a new sense of realism prevails among leading companies, most of whom have proved their point by being in a parlous financial state.

Unlike the Balance Sheet, the Profit and Loss Account reports on the organisation's activities over a particular period of time, although this in no way impairs imaginative construction. At the top of the P&L Account, as it is commonly called, the Total Sales for the period are given and from these figures are subtracted various costs such as Material, Wages, Heat and Light, and the Financial Director's old friend, Depreciation. In this way a Gross Profit is arrived at, and it is at this point that the Chairman leaps to his feet and directs that someone should arrange a three-week conference in Bermuda and someone else should place an order for an executive jet. The Financial Director then has to calm him down, lead him to a chair and carefully explain that the Overheads have still to be deducted, not to mention Corporation Tax and the final appropriations for Dividends and Reserves.

Once a year, the auditors descend on the company and go through everything with a fine toothcomb. However, judging by some of the financial shenanigans often brought to light subsequently by other means, one can only assume that a significant number of auditors know more about Mongolian yak farming than they do about accountancy. For the management fox no auditor should present a threat; apart from checking the arithmetic in the books (which you would gladly do for a quarter of the price), they won't do much more than count a few pieces of something in the stock-room. Unless the item is something very simple like a ball, you can show them almost anything and let them count to their hearts' content, as they will not have the remotest clue what a drop-forged helical widget is supposed to look like. In any event, they seldom choose an item with more than 25 to 30 pieces in the bin or on the shelf (which may well be indicative of their prowess as mathematicians!).

Once the auditors have given their seal of approval to an organisation's final accounts, they can be safely included, in skeleton form, in the annual report and employee newsletter. Here we have something of a contradiction in terms because in fact all the corporate skeletons are kept well hidden in the cupboard. Was the world and his wife informed about the horrendously expensive research and development programme which has produced no marketable results? And where was mention made of the mountain of products bought at a bargain price for a quick turnround, which are still clogging up the warehouse long after the market for them has gone? They will be difficult to find in the warehouse, as they will be hidden behind the three years' supply of stationery bought by the Purchasing Director during a supplier sales promotion so that he would be eligible for a week's free holiday in Paris. It's an ill wind that blows nobody any good.

THE BUDGET

The main area in which you will come up against corporate figuring is in the preparation and administration of budgets. The very mention of the word budget seems to strike fear into the hearts of some people, but there really is no need for the management fox to worry himself, as budgets are merely guesses based on last year's figures, and if it is only a guess, you can't be held responsible, can you? In fact, the process of setting budgets often takes the form of a jolly game, with departmental managers in budget committees sitting around a table making wild and unrealistic guesses as to the following year's performance (much in the same manner as brainstorming, q.v.), to the accompaniment of loud guffaws and the sound of betting money being slapped on the table. At the end of the session they emerge with the least hilarious solution and submit it as a budget. The boss then knocks fifteen per cent off the bottom line and tells the committee to recalculate the component parts; this having been carried out, everyone goes away happy that a workmanlike job has been done all round.

Considerable time can be saved in the process of setting a budget if the committee delegates one of its members to produce the budget by using the computer's random number generating facility (your accountant will certainly know if it has this facility, though he might not be willing to admit it). Very often budgets prepared in this way can claim equal if not greater accuracy than those compiled in the conventional arithmetic way.

The main purpose of budgets is to reassure all and sundry that precise forecasts have been made, taking every possible contingency into account, and that the enterprise will be run in a businesslike manner. Naturally this fools nobody except the very naïve, as the real purpose of budgets is to provide a testing ground for managers wherein they attempt to wangle more out of their budget than has been allowed. Three effective methods of achieving this are:

1) obtaining a purchase order number under false pretences so that when you use it to buy goods or services these will be charged to another manager's budget (similar to the method of charging drinks to a colleague's hotel room number without his knowledge)

2) putting the wrong code on supplier invoices so that your department doesn't get charged with them

3) having staff seconded to you from another department (and on its budget). When the pressure either to give them back or transfer them to your budget eventually becomes irresistible, you will, of course, inform the accounts departments to start charging them to you ... won't you?

When your boss tell you that it is time for you to prepare your budget for the following year, you will naturally go along to your sales department and ask them what they intend to sell, broken down by product groups, products and prices. When they have stopped laughing they will tell you that they have not got the remotest clue because:

— 'it's all in the lap of the gods'

- it depends on the economic climate, and if they could forecast that they wouldn't be in their present jobs
- they have no way of knowing the quantity, quality and price of rival products which might come on the market, and if they could forecast that ... etc.
- 'it's a new product'
- it all depends on the fluctuations in the Venezualan Bolivar and the political stability of the Turks and Caicos Islands
- the computer's sales analysis program is haywire and they couldn't even tell you how many they have sold this year

In these circumstances, manufactured products are usually the subject of three guesses, namely the Sales guess, the Production guess and the Distribution guess, which are pursued individually by departments in a competitive spirit that warms the heart of the Chairman.

The main steps you should take in preparing your budget are:

1) Take a guess as to the likely level of activity in your department.
2) If you are no good at guessing, ask the gateman or boilerman, as they usually are privy to the plans of top management and may be able to advise you.
3) Calculate and price your labour, materials and overhead requirements, allowing at least 30 per cent for inflation.
4) Add 20 percent for contingencies.
5) Add 20 per cent for 'buggerment factor'.
6) Add 10 per cent to allow negotiation with your boss.

Having submitted your budget, one of two things will happen. You will find out at some later date (when there is no chance of changing it) that your boss has arbitrarily lopped a large amount off the total or from individual items (you may find that although you have a budget to employ six new people you have no budget to train them); or your boss will call you to his office and go through your budget line by line, demanding a justification for everything. If this happens you'd better be prepared to do some fast talking, or failing all else, tell him that the spreadsheet on your computer is faulty and all the figures in the budget are rubbish. At this point you could offer to do a 'reverse' budget for him instead; that is, if he tells you the total

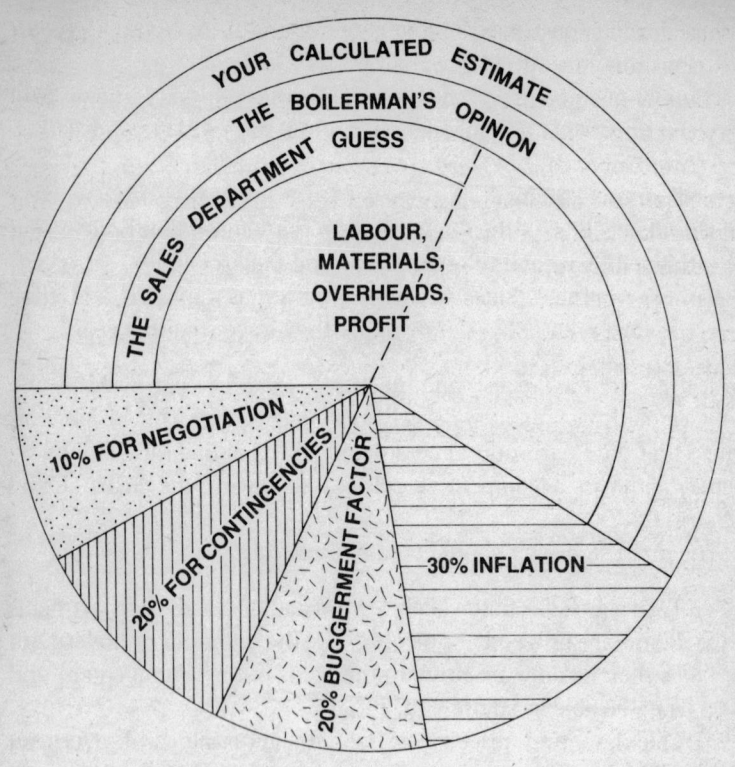

YOUR CALCULATED ESTIMATE

THE BOILERMAN'S OPINION

THE SALES DEPARTMENT GUESS

LABOUR,
MATERIALS,
OVERHEADS,
PROFIT

10% FOR NEGOTIATION

20% FOR CONTINGENCIES

20% BUGGERMENT FACTOR

30% INFLATION

monetary figure he is prepared to hand over for the running of your department next year, you can work it backwards by allocating varying amounts to each activity. In this way you will later be able to shuffle resources between activities, and as long as the total amount comes out about right your boss should have no room for complaint.

Naturally your boss will say that you must not overspend against your budget, or have too high a budget in the first place – what you do not know is that, while he takes an axe to your proposals (or rather *because* he takes an axe to them), he leaves his own well alone. This enables him to carry out vital and strategic projects such as redecorating the executive suite and taking a sales trip to Hawaii. While he is flying off around the world at the drop of an airline ticket, it would appear that, from the amount he has allowed for your essential travel, he expects you to walk everywhere and stay in youth hostels when you get there.

There is an increasing tendency for managers to get themselves personal computers so that they may bask in the reflected glory of these machines when it comes to matters financial. There they will sit all day merrily tapping away on their keyboards, feeding vital information into their databases, conversing brightly with their word processors and constructing such financial mazes on their spreadsheets that Albert Einstein might have found them difficult to decipher. Naturally the management fox will not fall victim to this piece of technological hokum as he knows that, having no glory of its own, all that a personal computer can reflect is the glory of its user; in other words, no glory, no reflection. This is apparent to all the computer whizz-kids (who could have done the calculations manually in a quarter of the time). One by one the screens darken and the dust upon them thickens. Thereafter the only characters to be seen on those screens will be where some wag has written, 'Do not remove: experimental dirt.' No, the management fox sees through all of this. He knows that spreadsheets and personal computers are wildly over-rated; when it comes to doing budgets there is only one tried and tested device which will do the job: the back of an envelope. He can only smile at his colleagues as they declare, 'We're right up at the front in the technology race: all our cock-ups are computerised. That's progress.'

With a little care and attention, there should never be any need for you to concern youself about figures in management; as with many other corporate subjects, if you appear to handle them with confidence and authority the actual figures you use are largely irrelevant, especially if you can throw in a few terms such as 'ratio', 'percentage' and 'standard deviation from the norm'. As all figures are relative, they have no meaning unless compared with last week's, last month's or last year's, so in most cases you can feel free to multiply by 4, divide by 2.8, or subtract the number you first thought of, as the notion takes you. By the time the accountants and directors have added a bit here, taken away a bit there, reapportioned and reallocated, the figures never bear much resemblance to reality anyway.

CONCLUSION

There is no doubt that if you decide to become a management fox you will have chosen a difficult path to follow, as you will be on your own and will rarely be able to turn to anyone else for assistance. Your greatest asset will be your freedom of action and the knowledge that management is a game which should not be taken too seriously, except in the matter of survival.

While the primary aim of becoming a management fox is to survive in the corporate jungle, there are other considerable benefits to be obtained, e.g.:

- there is scope for great initiative, as you are not constrained by things like fairness, honesty or integrity (though you may well ask who else in management feel themselves so constrained!)
- you will have the satisfaction of seeing managerial rivals crashing in flames, distracted by the apparent need to satisfy the capricious demands of staff, boss and customer
- you will be able to enjoy the satisfaction of a career spent pursuing the important management goals such as information-gathering, interpretation of rumours, laying traps for colleagues and taking advantage of malleable staff
- you will always have a known and constant code to follow and will be free of the ever-changing fads and fancies of the management theorists, which alone are enough to drive strong men to distraction

By using your foxy cunning you will be a survivor, observing the arrival and demise of the tigers and goats in the organisation, happy in the knowledge that, if you do ever fail in your quest, you never wanted the job in the first place. But the greatest satisfaction of all will come from being able to outsmart that self-satisfied smart-ass, the one minute manager! Now that you know how to do it, the rest is up to you.

GLOSSARY

APPLICATION FORM: an obstacle course designed to trap you into embarrassing admissions and omissions.

BOSS (foxes): the unspeakable in pursuit of the unbeatable.

BRAINSTORMING: a temporary seizure of the collective managerial grey matter, resulting in havoc.

BUDGET: a set of figures plucked from nowhere and going in a similar direction.

CAPITAL INVESTMENT APPRAISAL: using funny figures to justify an impulse buy by the chairman.

COMPUTER: an electronic number-cruncher which is responsible for at least 75 per cent of all corporate problems.

CORPORATE CULTURE: a kind of parlour game in which the chairman attempts to stamp the company name on the forehead of each employee.

CORPORATE PLANNING: the act of figuring it out, filing it and forgetting it.

DAMAGE LIMITATION EXERCISE: pulling your nuts out of the fire; a cover-up.

DECISION-MAKING: determining a course of action capable of being blamed on someone else.

DELEGATION: the distribution of responsibility to the needy.

EGOSPEAK: a technique used by experts: the deliberate use of words of which the listener is ignorant, in order to enhance the status of the speaker.

EXPERT: someone who knows more and more about less and less until he knows everything about nothing.

FAIRNESS: a quality much prized by goats but not generally exhibited by foxes.

FEEDBACK: a form of abuse given to a manager by his boss when a job goes wrong.

FORECASTING: using crystal balls to produce figures which are hocum.

INDUSTRIAL DEMOCRACY (or WORKER PARTICIPATION): anarchy.

INITIATIVE: a dangerous form of precociousness not to be encouraged in staff.

INTRAPRENEURING: 'looking for diamonds in the corporate navel and finding fluff'.

INVENTORY CONTROL: the Sales Prevention Department.

JOB DESCRIPTION: a fictional document specifically written for job interview purposes.

LEADER: the one with the arrows in his back.

MANAGEMENT BY WALKING AROUND: a moving target is harder to hit.

MANAGEMENT CONSULTANT: someone with a bag of solutions in search of a problem; a failed management lecturer.

MANAGEMENT FOX: a survivor; one who operates by stealth in the corporate jungle.

MANAGEMENT LECTURER: a failed manager.

MANAGEMENT THEORIST: an academic whose knowledge is untrammelled by practical management experience.

MANAGER: someone who has been unable to find a position as a management lecturer or consultant.

MANAGERIAL HALITOSIS: when a manager is on his way down – even his best friend won't want him to breathe a word of it.

MENTOR: a 'godfather' who will act as a raft to take you over the rapids.

MOTIVATION: the carrot or the stick; always take the carrot, as it will help you to see in the darkness of the corporate jungle.

OBJECTIVES: like New Year resolutions, a set of goals which are forgotten by 2 January.

ONE MINUTE MANAGING: here one minute...

ORGANISATION: a collection of people using the same route to achieve different goals.

ORGANISATION CHART: an accurate picture of the organisational structure four years ago.

PARTICIPATION: being allowed to have a say in irrelevant matters.

POLITICS: the interchange of ideas within an organisation; the main business of management.

PRAISE: a reward given to goats instead of money.

PRODUCTION CONTROL: a mythical land inhabited by deluded people whose output bears no resemblance to reality.

PROFIT: an excess of income over expenditure; not essential, but keeps the shareholders happy if achieved about once every three or four years.

PROMOTION: an attempt to turn a fox into a tiger; should be avoided at all costs.

SALES CONFERENCE: a meeting of light minds.

SELF-ACTUALISATION: if anyone ever knew what it meant it has long since been forgotten.

SEMINAR: what your boss goes to; you go on a training course.

SKUNK WORKS: these produce the expensive smell in the basement.

SYNERGY: two plus two equals five (will they please calculate your salary this way?).

SYSTEM: a series of instructions in a manual, the whereabouts and contents of which are unknown.

THEORY Z: perils of wisdom from the East; if this does not work then it is back to the beginning with Theory A.

TRAINING: an outmoded method of imparting knowledge to managers, now replaced by management development.

WRITTEN COMMUNICATIONS: hostages to fortune, to be avoided at all costs, except for personal defence.

INDEX